A Year Of Prosperity

52 Thoughts Concerning God's Design For Your Finances

a weekly devotional by
Heath Jarvis

For booking information and other Heath Jarvis
Ministries products, visit us on line at
www.HeathJarvis.com

ISBN: 1-59684-059-5

©Copyright 2005 by Heath Jarvis
All Rights Reserved
Printed by Derek Press, Cleveland, TN

Dedication

There are few times in a person's life when we meet someone who truly speaks into our life, irrevocably changing us for a lifetime. I can count on one hand the amount of people who fit that category—people who allowed God to use them to mold me into the man I am today.

For six years, I sat under the pastoral leadership of one such person. He is one of the finest teachers of God's Word that I have ever had the privilege of listening to. I say "finest" not because of his understanding of hermeneutics, nor of his knowledge of Greek and Hebrew, nor his eloquence of speech, but simply because of his understanding of God's character and how it pertains to our lives.

He is a man who has put God's Word into action in his own life, and achieved the results he sought. This is a man who was once in several thousands of dollars of debt. But he used Scriptural principles in his life to become debt-free. Now, he operates a company that helps people get out of debt. His company is blessed and prospered by God, making well into 7 digits per year. And on top of all of this, he is one of the finest husbands and fathers I have ever met.

I have used his example to pattern my life as a husband and father. I have applied his teachings to my ministry and my life decisions. I have seen God transform my life, my ministry, and my family as a result.

To the reader, I highly suggest his website: www.fflife.org

And to you, Pastor Gary Keesee, I dedicate this book. After all, most of the ideas presented are concepts I learned from you. God bless you, your family, your church, your company, and all of your endeavors ever abundantly.

For the furthering of the Kingdom,

A Year of Prosperity
Table of Contents

Introduction

Chapter 1 – You Were Born For Success 3

Chapter 2 – Robbing God 5

Chapter 3 – Benefits of the Tithe............................... 7

Chapter 4 – The Covenant of Prosperity 9

Chapter 5 – Overtaken by the Blessing – Part 1 12

Chapter 6 – Overtaken by the Blessing – Part 2 14

Chapter 7 – The Entity of Blessing 16

Chapter 8 – Sowing and Reaping............................... 18

Chapter 9 – Generous on Every Occasion 20

Chapter 10 – Money is Influence 22

Chapter 11 – The LAW of Sowing and Reaping............... 24

Chapter 12 – Men Will Give Unto You........................ 26

Chapter 13 – God Cares About the Fragments – Pt. 1 28

Chapter 14 – God Cares About the Fragments – Pt. 2 30

Chapter 15 – God Cares About the Fragments – Pt. 3 33

Chapter 16 – God Cares About the Fragments – Pt. 4 36

Chapter 17 – Being Debt-Free! – Part 1 38

Chapter 18 – Being Debt-Free! – Part 2 40

Chapter 19 – Turn Your Hurts Into Harvests 42

Chapter 20 – Don't Nullify Your Seed 45

Chapter 21 – Psalm 23 48

Chapter 22 – Assigning the Harvest to Your Seed 51

Chapter 23 – He Adds No Sorrow 53

Chapter 24 – More Than Enough 56

Chapter 25 – Redeemed From Moth and Rust 58

Chapter 26 – God is a God of Reward – Part 1 61

Chapter 27 – God is a God of Reward – Part 2 63

Chapter 28 – What is in Your Hand? 65

Chapter 29 – Praise and Giving 67

Chapter 30 – Paying Your Taxes 69

Chapter 31 – Pass the Biscuits 72

Chapter 32 – Can Rich People Enter Heaven? 74

Chapter 33 – Do Rich People Worship Money? 77

Chapter 34 – Does Money Make People Evil? 79

Chapter 35 – We Are God's Kids 81

Chapter 36 – Blessed to be a Blessing 83

Chapter 37 – The Gospel to the Poor.................................. 85

Chapter 38 – Our Daily Bread 87

Chapter 39 – Practical Principles Concerning Debt 89

Chapter 40 – God Wants to Meet All of Your Needs......... 92

Chapter 41 – God Wants to Meet All of Your Wants......... 94

Chapter 42 – Prosperity Flows Out of Marriage – Pt. 1 97

Chapter 43 – Prosperity Flows Out of Marriage – Pt. 2 99

Chapter 44 – Money Answers All Things 103

Chapter 45 – Uncap Your Potential!................................. 106

Chapter 46 – God Ideas.. 109

Chapter 47 – The Covenant of Faith – Part 1
"What Faith Is"... 112

Chapter 48 – The Covenant of Faith – Part 2
"What Faith Is Not".. 115

Chapter 49 – The Covenant of Faith – Part 3
"How Faith Works" 118

Chapter 50 – The Covenant of Faith – Part 4
"How Faith Is Built" 120

Chapter 51 – The Covenant of Faith – Part 5
"Faith and Works" 124

Chapter 52 – We Will Always Depend On God................ 127

Prosperity Scriptures 129

Introduction

The Word of God has much to say about our finances. There is a definite pattern established in Scripture concerning God's fiscal design for our lives. However, it seems that much of the Body of Christ does not understand God's character regarding money, which makes it perhaps one of the most misinterpreted concepts in the Bible.

I have a passion for seeing people walk in the fullness of God's will concerning their finances. In my local church, I am not only in charge of leading worship, but I also have the responsibility of receiving the Sunday morning offering. I use this opportunity to share with our people about Biblical concepts on finances, and so I would like to share these same life-changing concepts with you.

This book is designed as a weekly devotional. There are 52 chapters, making it a book that will take you through one year. Each chapter is relatively short so that you can use them for devotions of just several minutes.

My advice on how to read this book is to study one chapter per week. Try to apply the principles of that chapter to your life throughout the whole week. My suggestion is to read the same chapter (and the Scriptures associated with it) every day of that week, so as to keep the ideas fresh in your memory. Studies have shown that reading something just once usually results in a very small percentage of retention, if any at all.

You could read this book cover to cover in a short amount of time. But I believe that it would benefit you more to read it over a longer period of time so that you can slowly start applying these principles to your life. Applying these Biblical concepts will eventually become regular habits for you and your family.

My hope is that by the end of a year, you will have a new and fresh understanding of God's Character and His Will concerning you and your money. I further pray that in that time you will have established healthy fiscal habits and a pattern of success in your finances.

God is the giver of "good and perfect" gifts. He is a God of success, not failure. He is a God of provision and abundance. He desires to see us, His children, walk in victory in every area of our lives.

This book is ideal for anyone who wants to be debt-free, to live in God's provision and abundance, and it's for anyone who is tired of lack; everyone who wants the fullness of God's covenant with us. It is also a perfect book for Sunday school classes, devotional groups, cell groups or Bible studies. May this coming year be the season that financially turns your life around. God's best to you and yours as you seek His will.

Chapter 1

You Were Born For Success

What kinds of games did you play when you were a child? Guys, did you play "Cops and Robbers?" How about "Cowboys and Indians" or "King of the Hill?" Ladies, did you play "House?"

It is interesting that none of us ever played "Bankruptcy Court" or "Repo Day" as a child. None of us ever played "Debt Counseling," "Divorce Court" or even "Take the TV to the Pawn Shop." Why? Because we were born for success.

Failure is a learned behavior. If you observe children closely, you will notice that they do not understand when everything doesn't go their way. They don't play games expecting a loss or ones that ensure defeat. If they lose a race, they cry because they fully expected to win.

Fear is also a learned behavior. Most children will try anything at least once. I am a licensed pilot and my 4-year-old daughter loves to go flying with me. She loves to go up and down, loves to take steep turns and loves to be weightless. She is practically fearless. Some adults won't set foot in an airplane. Even though flying is statistically far safer than driving, adults have learned to fear flying, making flying the second most common fear among adults.

Success means having the courage, the determination, and the will to become the person you believe you were meant to be. – **George Sheehan**

A Year of Prosperity

To be successful will require courage. It will require determination. It will require will. And for a Christian, it also requires faith. Everything we receive in our covenant is received the same way, through faith. A simple definition of faith is "confident expectation." We can be "confidently expectant" that God will do what He said He would do...that He will be what He said He would be.

Romans 10:17 (KJV)
So then faith cometh by hearing, and hearing by the word of God.

Faith ultimately comes from the Word of God. If you want to build your faith regarding a certain subject or issue, you will need to find out what the Word says about that subject or issue. This book was written for the purpose of informing you about what God's Word says about your finances so that your faith can be built and you can freely receive God's promises concerning money.

Men are born to succeed, not fail – **Henry David Thoreau**

Now, even though we were born to become a success, we were not born successful. Consider this famous quote:

Successful people aren't born that way. They become successful by establishing the habit of doing things unsuccessful people don't like to do. The successful people don't always like these things themselves; they just get on and do them. – **Anonymous**

As you read and study this book, implement the ideas and practices of this book into your life until they become habits. The principles of this devotional book are based on the Word of God, a success book written by the most successful being in the Universe! And He created you for success as well!

Chapter **2**

<u>Robbing God</u>

The first thing we must understand about tithing and offering is that every mandate that God places on us is for our benefit. Every commandment, every law, every promise, every element of our covenant—they are all for our benefit as children of God.

> **Psalm 103:2 (KJV)**
> *Bless the LORD, O my soul, and forget not all his benefits.*

With God's benefits in mind, consider Malachi 3:8-9 (KJV):
[8] Will a man rob God? Yet ye have robbed me. But ye say, Wherein have we robbed thee? In tithes and offerings. [9] Ye are cursed with a curse: for ye have robbed me, even this whole nation.

Verse 8 says that if we don't tithe and give offerings, we rob God. But what do we rob Him of? Some would say, "we rob him *of* tithes and offerings." But the verse actually says we rob Him *in* tithes and offerings, not *of* tithes and offerings. God obviously does not need our money, so it is unreasonable to think that we have robbed him "of" the tithe and offering.

So the question still remains: What do we rob Him of? We rob Him of His ability to bless us. The tithe and offering are the devices that God has instituted to channel blessings into our life. God's plan for us is always goodness, provision, protection, blessing and abundance.

A Year of Prosperity

He wants nothing more than to bless us abundantly, but He will only bless us if we operate according to the pattern He established in Scripture. When it comes to our finances, that pattern is the tithe and the offering.

Notice that He also says that if we do not tithe and give offerings, we are cursed. God has no desire to place curses upon His people, but He is also bound by His own Word to lift His hedge of protection when we don't obey Him. If we are living under a curse, it is because we opened the door to it—not because God wanted to place a curse on us.

Don't rob God of His opportunity to channel blessings into your life. The tithe is for your benefit. Trust God with your finances by being faithful with the tithe.

Chapter 3

<u>Benefits of the Tithe</u>

Let us dig a little deeper into Malachi 3 to see some of the specific benefits of tithing.

> **Malachi 3:10-12 (KJV)**
> [10] *Bring ye all the tithes into the storehouse, that there may be meat in mine house, and prove me now herewith, saith the LORD of hosts, if I will not open you the windows of heaven, and pour you out a blessing, that there shall not be room enough to receive it.*
> [11] *And I will rebuke the devourer for your sakes, and he shall not destroy the fruits of your ground; neither shall your vine cast her fruit before the time in the field, saith the LORD of hosts.*
> [12] *And all nations shall call you blessed: for ye shall be a delightsome land, saith the LORD of hosts.*

First we see that one of the benefits of tithing is that it provides "meat" for the House of God. The church is the institution that has been ordained of God to receive the tithe and offering on behalf of God. Obviously, the needs of the church can be met through the tithe.

It is important to understand that it is the *church* that has been ordained by God Himself to receive our tithe. This means that our tithe, though it is given to a church, should be viewed as being given to God. It also means that when we try to manipulate churches and church leaders with our giving, this is an extreme insult to God. We should put our tithe in

A Year of Prosperity

the church and consider it released into the hands of God. What the church does with it is not our concern, for we will not have to answer to God for it.

Not only does it provide for the church we give into, but the tithe permits God to give into us. He opens up the heavens to pour us a blessing so large we cannot contain it. (Mal. 3:10)

We also see that God wants us to "prove" Him in this concept. This is the only place in Scripture where God asks us to put Him to the test. This is because He wants to channel blessings to us—so much that He begs us to take Him at His Word.

It further says that He will "rebuke the devourer". Satan would love nothing more than to devour you, your seed, your family and your provision. But God promises to intervene on our behalf so that the devourer cannot touch us. When the devourer is rebuked, it means that he cannot destroy our "fruits," which is symbolic of our provision and our labor. In other words, our labor will not be wasted, and our provision will always be there. This also means that our finances are protected and sanctified when we tithe.

The concept of our vine casting its fruit "before the time" is an agricultural concept. But I believe it also applies to our offspring. Because we tithe, our babies are carried to full term. I encourage those who are pregnant or wanting to conceive a baby to lay hold of this promise from the Word!

Finally, if our nation would obey the concepts of God, we would be blessed. Psalm 33:12 tells us that "blessed is the nation whose God is the Lord." A tithing nation will be a blessed and delightful land. America is blessed, not because it is a democracy, but because it was founded by Christians on Christian principles.

Release your faith as you tithe, and claim all of these promises for your own.

Chapter 4

The Covenant of Prosperity

Throughout Scripture we see examples of men who were blessed because of their relationship with God. Their covenant opened up blessings to them. Let's look at one such example:

Genesis 39:2-5 (KJV)

[2] And the LORD was with Joseph, and he was a prosperous man; and he was in the house of his master the Egyptian.
[3] And his master saw that the LORD was with him, and that the LORD made all that he did to prosper in his hand.
[4] And Joseph found grace in his sight, and he served him: and he made him overseer over his house, and all that he had he put into his hand.
[5] And it came to pass from the time that he had made him overseer in his house, and over all that he had, that the LORD blessed the Egyptian's house for Joseph's sake; and the blessing of the LORD was upon all that he had in the house, and in the field.

In verse 2 we see that the Lord was with Joseph and because of this, he was prosperous. At this time, he was still living in Egypt with Potiphar, having been sold into Egyptian slavery by his brothers. This shows that Godly prosperity is not affected by one's environment. Other men such as Abraham, Jacob and Job also prospered as a result of their covenant with God.

A Year of Prosperity

Verse 3 shows that Potiphar "saw" that the Lord was with Joseph. What did Potiphar see? Joseph's prosperity! God had prospered the work of Joseph's hand. Deuteronomy 28:10 says that, because of the blessing of the Lord on us, all nations will "see" that we are called by God. They will see the same thing Potiphar saw – our prosperity.

Because of God's hand on Joseph and his consequent success, Potiphar promoted him to overseer of his house. (Verse 4) The same thing happened to Daniel in Daniel 6, when Israel was under Babylonian captivity. King Darius made Daniel his chief president over the Kingdom. Isn't it amazing how ungodly people will promote godly people because of their success, but they won't accept their God?

In verse 5, we see that God blessed Potiphar on behalf of Joseph. God's blessing was on the entire estate of a pagan idol-worshipper, all because of *one man* who was in covenant with Him. This was not the first time that God blessed a pagan's house for the sake of someone who was in covenant with God. In Genesis 29-31, Laban's house was blessed on behalf of Jacob, even though Laban was a Syrian.

Even if you work for a secular institution, surrounded by unbelievers, do not fret. Your place of work will prosper simply because you are there. God will bless that business because He is in covenant with *you*—no matter what your environment! I have known several Christians (including my wife) whose secular workplaces prospered while they were there but began to dwindle after they left.

It is also interesting to note that Joseph managed to prosper throughout a drought in Egypt. Not only was Egypt able to withstand the drought, they were able to prosper in it. Nations had to come to Egypt to buy food, making Egypt the most prosperous nation on earth at the time. This shows us that our covenant grants us prosperity despite troubling economic circumstances. Your Covenant is not affected by the economy. Just as Joseph did, you can prosper through

A Year of Prosperity

difficult financial times. I have read that there were more millionaires created during the Great Depression than during any other era of our nation's history.

So don't let your station in life, your environment, or your economy discourage you from trusting God and believing Him to prosper you. He is bigger than all those circumstances. You have a covenant that will grant you prosperity; and it is God's good pleasure to bestow that prosperity upon you.

Chapter 5

<u>Overtaken by the Blessing Part 1</u>

One of God's greatest desires is to pour out blessings upon us. His character is one of reward, prosperity, provision and abundance. But He also requires obedience from His children. Deuteronomy 28:2-14 paints a picture of the blessing that God wishes to bestow upon us as reward for obedience. Let's start by looking at verse 2 through 8.

> **Deuteronomy 28:2-8 (KJV)**
> [2] *And all these blessings shall come on thee, and overtake thee, if thou shalt hearken unto the voice of the LORD thy God.*
> [3] *Blessed shalt thou be in the city, and blessed shalt thou be in the field.*
> [4] *Blessed shall be the fruit of thy body, and the fruit of thy ground, and the fruit of thy cattle, the increase of thy kine, and the flocks of thy sheep.*
> [5] *Blessed shall be thy basket and thy store.*
> [6] *Blessed shalt thou be when thou comest in, and blessed shalt thou be when thou goest out.*
> [7] *The LORD shall cause thine enemies that rise up against thee to be smitten before thy face: they shall come out against thee one way, and flee before thee seven ways.*
> [8] *The LORD shall command the blessing upon thee in thy storehouses, and in all that thou settest thine hand unto; and he shall bless thee in the land which the LORD thy God giveth thee.*

A Year of Prosperity

Notice (in verse 2) that blessings will "overtake" us if we obey God. Have you ever watched a race? Have you ever seen someone "overtake" another in the race? God is basically telling us that we won't be able to outrun our blessing if we are obedient!

Verse 3 shows us once again that our prosperity is not affected by our environment. Just as Joseph's prosperity was not affected by the fact that he was a stranger in Egypt, our prosperity will not be affected by whether we're in the city or in the field.

Verse 4 says the fruit of our body, our ground, our cattle, our kine (oxen) and our sheep will be blessed. You may remember that the fruit of our body (our offspring) was addressed in Malachi 3:11 where it says that our babies are carried to full term (our vine won't cast its fruit before the time). The fact that our ground and our flocks are blessed shows us that we won't have to waste our labor.

Our basket and store represent our provision. Baskets in this case were fruit baskets, and a "store" was a bread bowl. God is saying that we won't run out of food. In other words, He will provide our needs.

We will be blessed wherever we go, whether we are coming or going. And our obedience to God will grant us protection in our travels and against all of our enemies. He will also cause our enemies to be defeated "before" our face. We won't have to lift a finger because the battle is not ours, it's the Lord's. (2 Chronicles 20:15)

Modern-day examples of "storehouses" (verse 8) would be bank accounts and investments. Those will also be protected by God if we are obedient to Him. The work of our hands will be blessed and prosperous including our land.

Chapter 6

<u>Overtaken by the Blessing Part 2</u>

To continue our study on the blessings of Deuteronomy 28, let's look at verses 9-14 (KJV):

> [9] *The LORD shall establish thee an holy people unto himself, as he hath sworn unto thee, if thou shalt keep the commandments of the LORD thy God, and walk in his ways.*
> [10] *And all people of the earth shall see that thou art called by the name of the LORD; and they shall be afraid of thee.*
> [11] *And the LORD shall make thee plenteous in goods, in the fruit of thy body, and in the fruit of thy cattle, and in the fruit of thy ground, in the land which the LORD sware unto thy fathers to give thee.*
> [12] *The LORD shall open unto thee his good treasure, the heaven to give the rain unto thy land in his season, and to bless all the work of thine hand: and thou shalt lend unto many nations, and thou shalt not borrow.*
> [13] *And the LORD shall make thee the head, and not the tail; and thou shalt be above only, and thou shalt not be beneath; if that thou hearken unto the commandments of the LORD thy God, which I command thee this day, to observe and to do them:*
> [14] *And thou shalt not go aside from any of the words which I command thee this day, to the right hand, or to the left, to go after other gods to serve them.*

A Year of Prosperity

As presented in chapter 3 of this book, people will "see" that we belong to God because of our prosperity. The blessing that the Lord bestows upon us is what people will literally see. It is what Potiphar "saw" in Joseph...and according to verse 10, it is what all the people of the earth will see in us.

Verse 11 is somewhat of a reiteration of verse 4, but it also says we will be "plenteous" in goods. Plenteous means abundance and more than enough. God does not mind giving us more than we need, for He has more than enough to go around.

In verse 12, God's "good treasure" is His storehouse. Another translation is *armory*. In other words, God will hand us everything that is at His disposal. His storehouse is now our storehouse. Our crops will receive just the right amount of rain, and our labor will be blessed and not wasted.

Lending unto many nations and not borrowing (verse 12) means that we will be blessed to the point that we will not have to rely on debt to meet our needs. God's plan is for us to be debt-free.

What would you do if you knew you could not fail? What would you attempt if you knew that success was always guaranteed? Being the head and not the tail...above and not beneath...means that we will have the right to victory in every single area of our life. And all of this is because of our obedience to God. What awesome blessings He desires to shower us with!

We are the only ones who can hinder us from receiving these. Let us not cut off the covenant of prosperity through our disobedience. As one preacher once put it, "God will not bless you past your last act of disobedience." Obedience brings blessing that will "overtake" us!

Chapter 7

The Entity of Blessing

As we have seen in our recent look at Deuteronomy 28, blessings will "come on" us and "overtake" us if we obey God. And because of this obedience, God will "command" the blessing on our storehouses. In Psalm 133:3 we find that on Mount Zion, God "commanded the blessing".

These Scriptures almost make blessing sound like it is an entity in itself. When a blessing can "come on" you; "overtake" you; and be "commanded", it is almost as though blessing is a personality…a being.

Of course we know that blessing is not an actual being. But I believe that God was trying to show us a principle about how to operate as believers. Even though blessing is not an actual "being", we should still treat it as such.

When you pray over your finances, God wants you to exercise the authority you have as a believer. "Command" blessing as you would any person under your authority or jurisdiction. Make blessing obey your commands just as you would a subordinate. Order blessing to come upon you.

Blessing may not be an actual "entity"…but as Children of God with God-given authority, we should do as God does. Command the blessing into your life. Don't ask God to do it. He has already given the authority to you. Speak to it yourself just as though it were a person.

A Year of Prosperity

Command the blessing to come upon you and overtake you; command it to flow freely; welcome it into your life; speak to it and tell it to come on your finances, your family, your business, and the work of your hands. Then praise God for the authority He gives us as believers!

Chapter 8

Sowing and Reaping

If you study the parables of Jesus, you will find that He spoke about sowing and reaping more than any other subject. Over ½ of Jesus' parables addressed sowing and reaping in some manner. This means that not only did Jesus talk about sowing and reaping more than anything else...He talked about it more than everything else put together!

Many times we find that Jesus would start out a parable by saying, "A sower went to sow..." or "The Kingdom of Heaven is like a farmer who planted a mustard seed..." or "The Kingdom of Heaven is like a man who purchased a field..." Jesus had a lot to say about sowing and reaping.

> **2 Corinthians 9:6, 7 (KJV) says:**
> *6 But this I say, He which soweth sparingly shall reap also sparingly; and he which soweth bountifully shall reap also bountifully.*
> *7 Every man according as he purposeth in his heart, so let him give; not grudgingly, or of necessity: for God loveth a cheerful giver.*

This passage is talking about giving. The law of sowing and reaping states that what we make happen for others, God will make happen for us. What we give for the Kingdom, God will give back to us abundantly. If we sow sparingly, we will reap sparingly. The only person who can determine your harvest is you! Some people also refer to this as the law of reciprocity.

A Year of Prosperity

Every man should give what *he* decides to give. God may sometimes lay a certain gift on your heart...but most of the time, *we* will give what *we* decide. And the determining factor in how much we give is what kind of harvest we want to receive. We do not give begrudgingly or under compulsion. And we do not give because we have been manipulated to take care of a need or necessity. We give because we expect a harvest on seed sown.

Make all you can, save all you can, give all you can.
– John Wesley

The biggest motivation for your giving should be the return you expect. This is a foreign concept to many Christians, but God has absolutely no problem with "giving to get". Like all other elements of our covenant, this is a law that He established for *our* benefit. Receive it gladly because He wants you to! Put this law to work for you. If you have a need, sow a seed. And if you want an abundant harvest, sow an abundant seed.

By the way, God Himself used this law. God does not step outside of His own laws, His own statutes, or His own character. The Bible says in John 3:16 that "God so loved the world that He *gave* His only begotten son..." God wanted to reap millions of sons, so He sowed One! God wants us to use this law in the same way.

Chapter 9

Generous on Every Occasion

Let's continue our look at 2 Corinthians 9. We find that, as a result of our sowing:

> **2 Corinthians 9:11 (NIV):**
> *¹¹You will be made rich in every way so that you can be **generous on every occasion**, and through us your generosity will result in thanksgiving to God.*

If money were not an issue in your life, how would you live? What kind of house would you have? What kind of car would you drive? What would you do for your family? Where would you vacation? And most importantly, what would you do for others?

This passage tells us that money does not have to be an issue in our life. God wants to bless us to the point that we are able to be "generous on every occasion". How awesome would it be to be able to tell someone, "Don't worry about your rent this month, I'll take care of it." Or "You're having problems paying your taxes? Let me handle it." Further, how awesome would it be to be able to do this every time the need arises?

Of course we know that we could never be generous on every occasion unless all of our own needs were taken care of. To be able to be generous on every occasion requires an abundance of blessing and provision. And that type of blessing and provision is what God desires to bestow on us.

A Year of Prosperity

This passage also tells us that our generosity will result in people giving thanks to God. We are ambassadors of God's will in the earth. We are His agents, the ones who He uses to minister through, to speak through, to provide through. He wants to be able to provide people's needs through us.

This can be a tool for winning the lost as well! I know of people who have come to church because a Christian met a need of theirs. I know of a woman hairdresser who came to church and got saved after a Christian gave them a $100 tip for their haircut.

Our giving results in reaping an abundant harvest, which in turn grants us the ability to be generous on every occasion. In other words, we give to get so that we can give. And in giving we get so that we can give some more. On top of all of this, our giving results in people giving thanks to God. And in some cases, it will even be a catalyst for winning souls for the Kingdom of God. That's why the end of 2 Corinthians 9 (NIV) says:

[15]Thanks be to God for his indescribable gift!

What an indescribable gift is the law of sowing and reaping!

Chapter **10**

Money is Influence

> **Proverbs 14:20 (NIV):**
> [20] *The poor are shunned even by their neighbors, but the rich have many friends.*

Rich people are the most influential people in the world. Rich people control our economy. Rich people influence politics and fund campaigns. In our society, money is influence!

As ambassadors of Christ, we are the ones God has commissioned to carry out His Will in the earth. God wants us to be people of influence. Therefore He desires for us, His Children, to have the financial means to be influential in our society.

Let's talk about politics for a moment. Everyone remembers the 2000 Presidential Election between George W. Bush and Al Gore. The vote was so close that it took almost 6 weeks to determine the winner. But Bush and Gore were not the only people making the news during that election. You may remember that Ralph Nader was getting quite a bit of publicity at that time as well.

Ralph Nader was running for President, but he obviously knew that he would not win. So why did he run? Because there is a law that states that if you can get at least 5% of the popular vote, you are entitled to federal funds that you can use to run your next campaign. If Ralph Nader had gotten 5% of the popular vote (which he did not, by the way), he would

A Year of Prosperity

have received approximately $15 million in federal funds. I know that $15 million sounds like a lot of money. But when you consider that Bush and Gore each spent around $250 million, $15 million pales a little by comparison.

The point is this. How awesome would it be for the Body of Christ to be able to put a man in office...to be able to pool our resources together and tell a Godly man, "Here's $250 million. Go run yourself a campaign."?

You may say, "That's impossible!", but it would not have to start with the President. Christians could use their influence to elect mayors, local judges and sheriffs, state legislators, governors, and congressmen. We have a responsibility to see God's agenda carried out in politics. Voting is good, but it is just a start.

In 1976 the City of Cincinnati, Ohio passed a law that outlawed the buying or selling of pornography within their city limits. In 1997 Larry Flynt, editor of Hustler Magazine, managed to use his influence to get that law overturned. A 21-year law was overturned by one man of influence.

You see? The devil uses rich people to exercise influence for his kingdom. It's time for God's people to walk in the financial freedom and abundance that will give us the influence that God wants us to have in this world. He wants us rich because:

MONEY IS INFLUENCE!

Chapter 11

The LAW of Sowing and Reaping

God has established many laws in His Kingdom. There are physical laws and spiritual laws. Consider the law of gravity. It is a law that states that anything with mass attracts itself to anything else with mass...the more mass an object has, the more gravity it has.

The law of gravity is constant. It has never changed. It never will change. If you drop a ball from a 2nd story window, the ball will fall to the ground. It will always fall. If you try it tomorrow, it will fall. If you try it next week, next month, or even next year, it will always fall! The ball has no choice in the matter. Your emotions or circumstances will not affect the outcome. The ball must fall. Why? Because it is a law.

The law of sowing and reaping is also just that...a law. When you sow a seed, the seed has no choice but to produce. Your circumstances will not affect the outcome. Your seed must produce. Why? Because it is a law.

Imagine going back in time 150 years or so. Imagine telling someone from that time period that man would soon be able to fly in a machine that can carry hundreds of people at a time, and carry them thousands of miles at an altitude of over 35,000 feet at a speed of several hundred miles per hour. Imagine telling them that man would soon be able to leave this planet and land on the moon. Imagine telling them that man would soon be able to design a weapon that can destroy an entire city in a manner of seconds. They would probably

A Year of Prosperity

tell you that only God has that kind of power. They would probably think you were crazy.

In the late 1800s, there was a preacher who commonly preached that man had learned everything he was going to learn; man had advanced as far as he was going to advance; man had achieved, technologically, everything there was to achieve. That preacher from Ohio was Bishop Milton Wright. He had 2 sons, Orville and Wilbur. True story.

Laws like the law of lift and the law of atomic energy had always existed, but man had yet to discover them. We cannot tap into a law unless we know it exists. In the same way, a lot of Christians do not tap into the law of sowing and reaping because they do not know it exists. Many do not understand God as being One Who wants to provide all of our needs.

> **As Jesus said in John 8:32 (NIV):**
> *32Then you will know the truth, and the truth will set you free.*

The truth will set you free. What truth? The truth you know! Only the truth that you know can set you free...because only after you know of it can you tap into its power.

The Law of Sowing and Reaping is an immutable law; as immutable as the law of gravity. It is a law designed for our benefit. Use this law for your benefit. Your seed has no choice but to produce an abundant harvest because IT'S THE LAW!

> **Galatians 6:9 (KJV):**
> *In due season we SHALL reap, if we faint not.*

Why will we reap if we faint not? Because IT'S THE LAW!

Chapter 12

Men Will Give Unto You

Let's look at a very familiar verse of Scripture regarding giving:

> **Luke 6:38 (KJV):**
> *38 Give, and it shall be given unto you; good measure, pressed down, and shaken together, and running over, shall men give into your bosom. For with the same measure that ye mete withal it shall be measured to you again.*

If you read closely, you will see that it is men who will give unto you...not God. Ultimately, it is God that blesses us, but He will do it through men. I think sometimes Christians expect some mystical check to materialize or fall from the sky. But your blessing will actually come through men.

So many times we hear testimonies in church of how God brought unexpected checks to people or how someone stumbled on some unexpected money. God does bless us in those ways. But more often than not, He uses men to bless us. And most of the time the way we receive blessings through men is because of ideas that God gives *us*...not ideas that He gave to those men.

> **Consider what happened in Matthew 17:27 (NIV):**
> *27 But so we don't upset them needlessly, go down to the lake, cast a hook, and pull in the first fish that bites. Open its mouth and you'll find a coin. Take it and give it to the tax men. It will be enough for both of us."*

A Year of Prosperity

This is the story of how Jesus showed Peter how to pay his taxes. He told Peter to go catch a fish, and use the coin in the fish's mouth to pay their taxes.

Coins are not minted in Heaven. They are minted on earth. The coin that Peter found had once belonged to someone. In other words, a *man* had to lose that coin in order for Peter to find it. Perhaps a fisherman or pleasure boater accidentally dropped the coin in the water. Perhaps someone crossing over to the other side tossed the coin in and made a wish. However it happened, God knew where the money was. God led Peter to his provision, but ultimately his provision came through men.

> **Proverbs 13:22 (KJV) tells us that:**
> [22b] *The wealth of the sinner is laid up for the just.*

We should not consider it any less miraculous, any less supernatural that our blessing comes from a man. Do not feel ashamed to receive blessings from men. When a man wants to bless you...when a man wants to give you business...when a sinner loses finances and you gain them...consider that a blessing from God!

Chapter **13**

God Cares About the Fragments
Part 1

There are two different instances in the book of Mark where Jesus preached to a multitude and then used a miracle to feed them. Let's look at both of those stories:

> **Mark 6:41-43 (KJV)**
> *41 And when he had taken the five loaves and the two fishes, he looked up to heaven, and blessed, and brake the loaves, and gave them to his disciples to set before them; and the two fishes divided he among them all.*
> *42 And they did all eat, and were filled.*
> *43 And they took up TWELVE BASKETS full of the FRAGMENTS, and of the fishes.*

> **Mark 8:7, 8 (KJV)**
> *7 And they had a few small fishes: and he blessed, and commanded to set them also before them.*
> *8 So they did eat, and were filled: and they took up of the broken meat that was left SEVEN BASKETS.*

Shortly after this instance in Mark 8, Jesus reminded the disciples about both accounts:

Mark 8:19-21 (KJV)

[19] *When I brake the five loaves among five thousand, how many baskets full of FRAGMENTS took ye up? They say unto him, Twelve.*
[20] *And when the seven among four thousand, how many baskets full of FRAGMENTS took ye up? And they said, Seven.*
[21] *And he said unto them, How is it that ye do not understand?*

What is a "fragment?" A fragment is that thing which is of little or no value to the person who possesses it. So because it is of no value, they discard it. When these people were hungry, they would have considered every morsel extremely valuable. But since they were filled and satisfied (Mark 6:42; Mark 8:8), they discarded the fragments.

The interesting thing to note is how much was gathered. In one case, they gathered 12 baskets. In the other case, 7 baskets were picked up.

What are the fragments in your life? What are the things that you do not mind discarding because they are so small? For what services and products do you overpay? What fragments could you gather? Sometimes, by good stewardship, we may only pick up $1 here, $5 there, $3 here, $10 there. But sooner or later, those fragments will add up to 7 or 12 baskets full.

Most people have areas where they can trim their spending. In the next 3 chapters, we will look at practical ways to gather our fragments.

Chapter **14**

God Cares About the Fragments Part 2

In the previous chapter, I shared with you the concept of gathering the fragments, according to the stories from Mark 6 and Mark 8. What are the *fragments* in your life? What things do you discard as being of no value? Where do you overspend for products and services? The following are examples of things you can do to help gather the *fragments*. I highly suggest that you try to find at least 1 fragment in this chapter that you can gather.

- Insurance – Many people have the wrong kind(s) of insurance. Many have more insurance than they need. The average person in the U.S. keeps their car insurance company for over 16 years. This means people are not taking the time to see if there are any better rates out there. And insurance companies and insurance salesmen are making more money than ever!

- Long Distance Phone Service – Many people do not bother to find the best plan that is out there for them. There is much competition between long-distance carriers. You may have the wrong plan for your needs. Also, some calling cards out there are as little as 2 to 3 cents per minute. The competition between communications companies means money in the pockets of smart consumers.

A Year of Prosperity

- Cell Phone – Here again, companies are extremely competitive. New types of plans are being offered all the time. Louise and I recently switched plans and got a better phone, a better plan, AND saved $40 per month! All it cost us was the time to go to the mall and switch plans.

- Interest rates – Interest rates were slashed after 9/11 due to the need to strengthen the economy. Did you take advantage of those rates? Louise and I bought a van at 0% interest. Our mortgage loan is at 4.6%. As I write this, rates are starting to climb again. If you want to save some money, you may want to refinance quickly before the rates climb much more. Many times, the refinance fee can be paid off in a matter of just several months.

- Eating out – I do not have to tell you that eating out is much, much, more expensive than eating in. My wife, Louise loves Italian food. She recently bought a frozen Chicken and Broccoli Fettuccine Alfredo meal kit that feeds 3 to 4 for only $3.96! It tasted great and took only 15 minutes to prepare in a skillet. And sometimes cooking from scratch is even cheaper than buying ready-made meals. What cost us less than $4 would have cost over $20 at Olive Garden.

- Unused services and other items – It is not necessary to pay for cable TV if you do not watch TV. Or to buy season tickets if you only go to 1 or 2 games a year. Or to subscribe to magazines or newspapers that you do not read. Or to pay monthly fees for fitness clubs that you do not attend. Or to buy movies that you will only watch once when you could rent them for much less. Find out what your unnecessary expenditures are. Those are fragments!

- Energy – This falls under the category of paying for stuff you don't use. If you walk out of a room...turn

A Year of Prosperity

the lights out, turn the TV off, etc. If you are not going to be home, adjust your thermostat to save energy. If you are home at night, turn your outside house lights off. If you are sitting in a parking lot, shut your car off. Do not pay for energy you are not using.

In the next two chapters, we will look at even more ideas for gathering fragments.

Chapter **15**

God Cares About the Fragments Part 3

Hopefully, you found at least 1 fragment in the last chapter that you were able to gather. Let's see if you can gather another 1 (or more) in this chapter. Here are some more fragment-gathering ideas:

- Buy in Bulk - Several years ago, I was asked by my manager to go to an office store to buy some supplies. One thing we needed was floppy disks. The store had a 10-pack for $10, and a 50-pack for $25. My manager told me to buy the 10-pack because, "It's cheaper, and we don't need 50 floppy disks." I replied, "Will you ever use 50 floppy disks in the history of this operation? If so, then let me buy the 50-pack because they are by far the better buy." He told me to stay with the 10-pack. There is an old saying that I have heard that accurately described that manager: *penny-wise and pound-foolish*. Sam's Club and other types of membership warehouses are ideal places for buying in bulk.

- Don't Buy New Cars - New cars depreciate about 40% the moment they're driven off the lot. You can save yourself a lot of money by buying a car that is 1-3 years old, especially if it is still in warranty. Louise and I bought a 2000 model van in 2001 with 23,000 miles on it. Sticker prices on new vans were at $26,000, and the book value for the used van we were buying was

$20,000. We bought our van for only $15,300! And we still had the remainder of a 75,000 mile warranty.

Our next vehicle purchase was a brand new van that was part of a hail damage sale. It had a few dents on one fender, on the hood, and on the roof. The sticker price on it was $33,000 but we paid only $18,000! We still got the full warranty on a van with only 90 miles on it. Plus, we put down a few thousand dollars and financed the rest at 0% interest.

- **Don't Buy *Junk* Cars** – Consider this when buying a used car. It does not matter that the car only costs $500 when it costs $100 per month to repair and maintain. Don't let cars *nickel-and-dime* you. Those *nickels* and *dimes* are fragments!

- **Avoid Traffic Tickets** – This was a fragment of mine in years past. Parking tickets, speeding tickets, etc. will really add up quickly. Most speeding tickets start at no less than $90, and some can soar above $200! Slow down, get up half an hour earlier, plan ahead…do whatever you need to do to avoid this unnecessary expenditure.

- **Buy Less Expensive Clothing** – The mark-up on new clothing prices is probably more than most people think. Some places mark-up clothing as much as *10 to 20 times* their cost! Some stores buy overstock from other stores and sell it for a small fraction of the cost of the department stores. I shopped at one such store not long ago and witnessed a woman buying three suits for her husband for $80! Some outlet stores also have great prices on clothing.

- **Be Selective with Brand Names** – Sometimes brand names are important; sometimes they are not. If you can do without the name, you usually can save quite a bit of money buying a generic brand. I do not like

A Year of Prosperity

some generic foods, but some are all right. Our family almost exclusively uses generic medicines and vitamins. I usually buy brand name shoes because they are more comfortable and last longer. But I am a little less demanding about shirts and pants. Find out what brand names you can live without.

We will finish these thoughts on fragments in the next chapter.

Chapter 16

God Cares About the Fragments
Part 4

Here are some final thoughts on ways to gather fragments:

- Buying on Sale – One day I walked out of a gas station/convenience store after buying a bag of chips that cost well over $3! Those same chips are normally on sale at Wal-Mart for $1.50, plus the bag is even bigger! I walked out of that convenience store saying to myself, "Well, there went a fragment." It would have only taken about 5 more minutes to get the chips at a less expensive store.

- Coupons – Many stores offer double coupons. Sure it takes time to clip them, but it is not hard to pick up as much as $20 or even much more in savings. Many stores have great mark-downs on certain products just to get you in the store. Couple those deals with double coupons, and sometimes you can get items for free…or even *less than* free! That's right! You can even get stores to pay you for buying their products!

- Don't Pay for the Last-Minute Rush – This was a particular fragment that Louise and I had to work at to gather it. Lack of planning ahead often caused us to pay rush fees. Fed Ex often charges 5-6 times more for overnight delivery than regular shipping. Don't pay rush fees for your paid services. Rush fees are definitely fragments.

A Year of Prosperity

- Bank Fees – Banks are also becoming more and more competitive. Many banks offer free checking, accounts with no fees for money orders and cashier's checks, or accounts with no ATM fees. It would be to your advantage to scout around and see if there are banks out there with better deals than your current bank. Perhaps even your current bank has accounts that are better suited to your needs and can save you on fees.

  While we are on the subject of banks, consider this: Many people have accounts through their employer's credit union—or something similar—that may not have any fees. But if your bank is not nearby, you may have to pay ATM fees to visit the bank(s) closest to you. Switching to a closer bank may not only save you on gas, but ATM and other fees as well. Those fees are fragments.

  Finally, concerning bank accounts, Christians need to be responsible with their money. Not keeping a balanced account puts you at risk of overdrawing your account and being charged overdraft fees. Many times these fees are well over $20 per check. This type of money is too large to be considered a fragment! Be responsible with your money so you will not be charged these astronomical fees. And stay away from those "check-cashing" places. Their interest rates are just so outrageous. If you are responsible with your money, you will not need to use those places anyway.

If you are married, sit down with your spouse and discuss these ideas. Sure, you may only save $1 here, $5 there, $10 there, and $8 there, but when you put them all together, you'll end up with 12 baskets full. Do not consider a fragment to be of no value just because it is small. You will be amazed at how much you can save with a little discipline. Eventually you will find this discipline a regular habit...and that is responsible stewardship!

Chapter 17

Being Debt-Free!
Part 1

Deuteronomy 15:6 (KJV)
[6]For the LORD thy God blesseth thee, as he promised thee: and thou shalt lend unto many nations, but thou shalt not borrow; and thou shalt reign over many nations, but they shall not reign over thee.

Deuteronomy 28:12 (KJV)
[12] The LORD shall open unto thee his good treasure, the heaven to give the rain unto thy land in his season, and to bless all the work of thine hand: and thou shalt lend unto many nations, and thou shalt not borrow.

Proverbs 22:7 (KJV)
[7] The rich ruleth over the poor, and the borrower is servant to the lender.

God makes it pretty clear in the Bible that He wants His children debt-free. Debt is extremely debilitating, demoralizing, and inhibiting. But as debilitating as debt is, being debt-free is just as liberating—if not more so!

Consider this example: If you have a $121,000 loan at 10% interest, and you are paying $1,000 a month on your loan...YOU WILL NEVER PAY OFF THAT LOAN!!! The

A Year of Prosperity

interest on $121,000 at 10% comes to $12,100 per year. $1,000 per month will only come to $12,000 per year...not enough to cover the interest on the loan, let alone any principal.

Now consider this: If you are debt-free and are able to set aside $1,000 a month and can invest that money at 10% interest, you can save that same $121,000 in LESS THAN 7 YEARS! Same amount of money, same monthly payment, same interest rate...completely different result.

Now, I realize that 10% is a high rate for an investment. And I know that most $121,000 loans don't have rates as high as 10%. But that's not the point. The point is to show a comparison using the same amounts of money, to illustrate how important it is to keep your money in your own hands. Can you see how liberating it is to have your money working for you? Banks want your money to work for *them*. Banks and finance companies are making money *hand-over-fist* from people who voluntarily sell themselves into poverty and slavery.

Consider how easy is it to get a credit card, even if you have bad credit. Many finance companies offer loans at well over 20% interest! This type of debt is financially destroying people. Christians need to be debt-free. Christians will never be able to be "generous on every occasion" or have "influence" unless they are free from their debt.

As we continue, we will look at different tips on becoming debt-free. You will find that it is easier than you think to be debt-free without changing your income. Ask God to show you how to get started in this process. It is His desire to see you debt-free, so be assured that He will show you how to do it by His Spirit. You can be debt-free!

Chapter 18

Being Debt-Free!
Part 2

"How can I be debt-free?" you may be asking. One of the ways you can start is by taking the "fragments" that you have gathered from chapters 13 through 16 of this book, and applying that extra cash flow toward your debt. 12 baskets of fragments can go a long way in starting down the road to financial freedom.

The first thing you should do in becoming debt free is to destroy your credit cards. In other words, cut off the source. If you do not have credit cards, you cannot let them pull you deeper into debt.

You should also repent to God and ask for His forgiveness for relying on debt as your source, rather than Him. He says that He will supply all of your needs (Philippians 4:19). He says that if we seek Him first, our needs will be added to us (Matthew 6:33). Turn from using debt as your supply, and ask God to help you become debt-free.

Next, you should establish a cash reserve. Set back a few thousand dollars for emergencies. You never know if your car will need new tires, if a refrigerator will quit working, or if some other unexpected expenditure will arise. Having a cash reserve will negate the impulse of turning to your credit card to take care of those needs. You can use your fragments to help establish that cash reserve.

A Year of Prosperity

Now that you have a cash reserve, you can start working off your debt. A great place to start is by continually applying your fragments toward paying off your credit cards or other high-interest debt. In most cases, your largest interest rates should be eliminated first. They are the most debilitating. You may want to first see if you can consolidate your high-interest debt into a lower-interest rate like a home equity loan or a lower-interest credit card. But do not open up another credit card account to do this.

After your credit cards or finance company loans are paid off, you can take the money you were using to pay those monthly payments, plus your fragment money, and start applying it to your car loan(s) or your equity loan. And after those are paid off, you should have a hefty amount of money per month to start applying toward your mortgage.

Remember this, too. Aside from your cash reserve, it makes very little sense to have a bunch of money saved in low-interest accounts like CDs and savings accounts, when you still owe money on higher-interest loans. For example, if you owe $10,000 on a credit card with 11% interest and have $10,000 in a CD making 5% interest, you're just losing money. Take the money out of the CD and pay off your credit card.

As we saw in the previous chapter, having debt is extremely debilitating just as being debt-free is extremely liberating. Get your debt paid off first, *then* you can get to work on investing and saving…letting your money work for you!

God wants you out of debt. God wants you in control of your destiny. God wants you to live in abundance. God wants you to be able to be "generous on every occasion." With His help, you can and *will* defeat this monster…this devourer…called debt!

Chapter 19

Turn Your Hurts Into Harvests

> **Luke 6:27-35 (NIV)**
> [27]*But I tell you who hear me: Love your enemies, do good to those who hate you,*
> [28]*Bless those who curse you, pray for those who mistreat you.*
> [29]*If someone strikes you on one cheek, turn to him the other also. If someone takes your cloak, do not stop him from taking your tunic.*
> [30]*Give to everyone who asks you, and if anyone takes what belongs to you, do not demand it back.*
> [31]*Do to others as you would have them do to you.*
> [32]*If you love those who love you, what credit is that to you? Even 'sinners' love those who love them.*
> [33]*And if you do good to those who are good to you, what credit is that to you? Even 'sinners' do that.*
> [34]*And if you lend to those from whom you expect repayment, what credit is that to you? Even 'sinners' lend to 'sinners,' expecting to be repaid in full.*
> [35]*But love your enemies, do good to them, and lend to them without expecting to get anything back. Then your reward will be great, and you will be sons of the Most High, because he is kind to the ungrateful and wicked.*

I have already stated that Jesus spoke about sowing and reaping in more than half of his parables. Here is yet another example of a teaching on sowing and reaping. Some people have interpreted this passage to mean that Christians should be a bunch of pushovers—that Christians should be

doormats for others to walk on. But that is not the point that Jesus was trying to make.

Jesus was saying that if people do bad things to you, you could retaliate...but what good would it do you? Sure, you can try to obtain justice in your own strength. But God can do so much more on your behalf than you could ever do on your own. And on top of this, if you let *God* do it for you, He says it will be added to your "credit" and your "reward." In other words, Jesus was saying that if someone steals from you or does something bad to you, just consider it seed sown. Then expect and receive a harvest on the seed you have sown. The harvest you receive will be so much more than what you could obtain by your own efforts.

This goes further than simply releasing someone from an obligation or debt owed to you. You need to actually "sow" what that person stole from you. It is a mind-set, an attitude of the heart. It says that not only are you releasing them from what they did to you, but you are gladly sowing what was stolen so that you can gladly receive the harvest.

Someone once promised to pay me over $4,000 for services rendered. For over 5 months, repeated phone calls went unreturned. I received several empty promises of checks "in the mail" and received nothing from him—not even a dime! After over 5 months of this, I ran into him at a church service. The first thing he started to do was make excuses as to why he had not fulfilled his promise. I did not let him finish his excuses...I simply released him from his obligation. At that moment, he got somber and said, "Heath, you have a lot more integrity than most men." Less than a month later, I received the best job I ever had. God has blessed me so abundantly since that time.

A friend of mine had an incident at his workplace where a co-worker unjustly caused him to be demoted. The demotion cost him over $5,000 in yearly salary. My advice to him was

A Year of Prosperity

to consider it seed sown. The harvest on a $5,000 seed is much more abundant than any retaliation he could attempt.

So start sowing your hurts. The devil will come to realize that every time he tries to steal from you, you just end up sowing it as seed, receiving a bigger harvest. By doing so, you will turn your hurts into harvests!

Chapter 20

Don't Nullify Your Seed

Galatians 6:9 (KJV)
And let us not be weary in well doing: for in due season we shall reap, if we faint not.

We have already established that the Law of Sowing and Reaping is as immutable as the Law of Gravity or any other law that God has established in His Kingdom. But we do see that there is an "if" in the above Scripture. There are things that can nullify your seed. One of those things is "fainting."

We know that we will reap in due season if we don't faint. But what does it mean to faint? The Greek word from which it is translated means *to weaken* or *become enfeebled*. It also means *to loose* or *to set free*. In other words, it means to let go of what you are standing on, to release what you have already claimed for yourself.

How do we faint? One of the most common ways is by our confession. Many people lose heart, and therefore they lose their confession of faith. After releasing their seed in faith, they forget about God's promises...they become disheartened; they wish they had their seed back. It is much the same as a farmer who plants his seed, then digs it back up. If the seed cannot take root in good soil, if it cannot be watered and nurtured, or if it cannot be allowed to grow on it's own, it will never produce.

Proverbs 6:2 says that we are "snared by the words" of our mouth. Proverbs 18:21 says that "Death and life are in the

45

A Year of Prosperity

power of the tongue." Jesus said in Matthew 12:34 that "out of the abundance of the heart" our mouth speaks. The confession of our mouth, which is evidence of what we believe in our heart, is full of power and authority. And it will either bring death or life to our situation.

Proverbs 23:7 says that as a man "thinketh in his heart, so is he." This is because out of the abundance of his heart, he will speak. And what he speaks brings death or life. This is why Proverbs 4:23 tells us to guard our heart, for out of it flow the "issues of life." What do these *issues* flow through? They flow through our mouth!

Notice that Proverbs 4:23 does not tell us to guard our mouth. That is because if we guard our heart, our confession will follow. Keep your heart full of faith by staying in the Word. Faith is always based on the Word—and based on the Word only. Do not lose your faith, and do not lose your confession.

Negative confessions that discouraged people find themselves saying:

"Well, if it would happen to anyone it would happen to me..."

"Man, my head is killing me!"

"I don't know how we're going to pay our bills this time...we might not make it..."

"This restaurant always messes up my order!"

"What's the worst that could happen?"

"Maybe this faith thing doesn't work..."

You have sown a seed. The Law of Sowing and Reaping says that the seed MUST produce a harvest. You WILL reap in due season if you faint not. Believe it! Receive it by faith! Trust

A Year of Prosperity

God! Keep your confession of faith based on God's Word. Don't nullify your seed.

Also, don't forget about your past seed sown from which you have yet to receive a harvest. Some of us have even sown seed that we have forgotten about. But continue to water your seed with the Word of God. Write down and document the different times you have sown seed as you believed God for your harvest. Your seed **WILL** produce. It has no choice!

Chapter 21

Psalm 23

Psalm 23 is one of the most popular chapters in the Bible. It is commonly used in funerals, and because of this, it is usually viewed as a very somber chapter of Scripture. However, I believe it is actually a celebration of the provision of God.

David, the writer of Psalms, held many occupations in his lifetime. He was a king, a warrior, a singer, instrumentalist and songwriter; and early in life he was a shepherd. In this particular Psalm, he chose to compare God to the attributes of a shepherd by using shepherding terminology.

Psalm 23:1
The Lord is my shepherd; I shall not want.

When I was growing up, I was told that this verse meant that we were not allowed to want; that we were not allowed to have desires. But what it actually means is that because God is our shepherd, our Provider, we will never *be in want*—or lack.

Psalm 23:2
He maketh me to lie down in green pastures: he leadeth me beside the still waters.

Just as a shepherd leads his flock to their provision, God leads us to ours. Notice that we can "lie down" in these pastures. Have you ever seen a sheep eat while lying down? Sheep normally eat standing up. David is saying that we will

A Year of Prosperity

have so much provision that we can lie down in it...we don't have to work for it. Also, the fact that they are "green" pastures and "still" waters tells us that when God has a choice, He give us the best that is available.

<u>Psalm 23:3</u>
He restoreth my soul: he leadeth me in the paths of righteousness for his name's sake.

God has something at stake here. He is concerned about His Name's sake. He never wants it to be said that He failed to provide for one of His own. Your prosperity is a testimony of God's goodness to men. He blesses us for so many reasons; one of those reasons is that He gets glory for His Name's sake!

<u>Psalm 23:4</u>
Yea, though I walk through the valley of the shadow of death, I will fear no evil: for thou art with me; thy rod and thy staff they comfort me.

Up until this verse, David has talked about how *God* is our shepherd:
- *He* makes us lie down
- *He* leads us beside still waters
- *He* restores our soul
- *He* leads us in righteousness for *His* Name's sake.

Now, David switches gears and says, "though *I* walk through the valley..." David understood that *God* does not lead us into dark places...we do that ourselves. But even when we are there, we take comfort in knowing that God never leaves us or forsakes us. (Hebrews 13:5) And David also took comfort in God's rod and staff, the instruments of correction, because he knew that God's correction would get him out of the dark place and back on the path to righteousness, goodness and provision.

A Year of Prosperity

Psalm 23:5

Thou preparest a table before me in the presence of mine enemies: thou anointest my head with oil; my cup runneth over.

The image of a table is another picture of provision—a chance for God to show off His goodness. God prepares a meal for us right in front of the devil, our enemy! And for spite's sake, He anoints us and fills our cup to overflowing right in our enemy's face!

In ancient days, when a visitor came to someone's house, it was considered an extreme insult to not invite them in and offer them something to drink. But it was also understood by the visitor that they were supposed to leave after their drink was finished. So if their drink was refilled, it was perceived that they were welcome to stay awhile. Here, David shows us that our drink is not only refilled...it is filled to overflowing! God is a God of overflow—a God of exceeding abundance.

Psalm 23:6

Surely goodness and mercy shall follow me all the days of my life: and I will dwell in the house of the LORD for ever.

There are those who say that we are only promised prosperity, healing, blessing (the goodness of God) in the afterlife. They say that we are not promised these things on earth. This verse clearly tells us that we can have these things here on earth as well as in Heaven. After a life full of God's goodness and mercy, we can enjoy being in the Presence of the Lord forever!

Chapter 22

Assigning the Harvest to Your Seed

Genesis 1:11-12 (KJV)
*[11] And God said, Let the earth bring forth grass, the herb yielding seed, and the fruit tree yielding fruit **AFTER HIS KIND**, whose seed is in itself, upon the earth: and it was so. [12] And the earth brought forth grass, and herb yielding seed **AFTER HIS KIND**, and the tree yielding fruit, whose seed was in itself, **AFTER HIS KIND**: and God saw that it was good.*

We've talked a lot in this book about sowing seed. We see in these verses that seed was designed to produce after its kind. Luke 6:38 tells us that if we give, "it" shall be given unto us. So, what is "it?" "It" is whatever we give.

There is a principle in God's Word that states that whatever we make happen for someone else, God will make happen for us. It is commonly referred to as the Law of Reciprocity. If you need a healing, pray for someone else's healing. If you welcome a prophet, you will receive his reward. Seed produces after its kind.

I have a friend named Jeff. Jeff is a father of four girls, (ages 2 to 11) and he is an avid golfer. I have another friend named Joel. Joel is a teenager and is also an avid golfer. Both men—mutually acquainted—are Christian men of great character and conviction whom I respect very much.

A Year of Prosperity

One day Jeff decided to bless Joel with an expensive golf club. He did this because he saw a tremendous amount of godly attributes in Joel and wanted to sow into a godly young man. Jeff did this as a point of contact to release his faith and believe God for four godly young suitors for his daughters. He knew that if he sowed *into* a godly young man, in time he would reap four godly young men for his girls when they reached an appropriate age. And his only purpose in blessing Joel was to believe God for this.

Jeff forgot something, though. He forgot that seed reproduces after its kind. All he was believing God for was four godly men for his daughters. But what he *sowed* was a golf club. And a golf club sown reaps a golf club. A few weeks later, Jeff was at a country club and was entered into a drawing for a brand new set of very expensive clubs. Of course he won those clubs because seed reproduces after its kind. His golf club was returned in good measure, pressed down, shaken together and running over!

If you need a car, buy someone a tank of gas, or change their oil for them. If you need clothes, give some clothes away. If you need a house, pay someone's rent for them, or go help someone paint their kitchen. If you have a need, sow a seed.

The wonderful thing about money is that it represents so many things. Money buys cars. It buys clothes. It pays rent. It pays taxes. It pays doctor bills. It buys braces for your children's teeth. As Ecclesiastes 10:19 says, it "answers all things." Money can be used as a seed sown for anything because it represents "all things."

Since money can be used as a seed for whatever you want or need to assign as your harvest, you can sow money as a seed and believe God with confident expectation for your harvest. Know that the seed you sow in faith will reproduce after its kind. As you sow, speak over your seed and assign it to your harvest!

Chapter 23

He Adds No Sorrow

Proverbs 10:22 (KJV)
²²*The blessing of the LORD, it maketh rich, and he addeth no sorrow with it.*

Most theologians and Bible scholars believe that the "blessing of the Lord" in various passages of the Old Testament refers to the blessing of Abraham. This is significant because Abraham was an extremely wealthy man. We read this in Genesis 13:

Genesis 13:5-9 (NIV)
⁵ *Now Lot, who was moving about with Abram, also had flocks and herds and tents.*
⁶*But the land could not support them while they stayed together, for their possessions were so great that they were not able to stay together.*
⁷*And quarreling arose between Abram's herdsmen and the herdsmen of Lot. The Canaanites and Perizzites were also living in the land at that time.*
⁸*So Abram said to Lot, "Let's not have any quarreling between you and me, or between your herdsmen and mine, for we are brothers.*
⁹*Is not the whole land before you? Let's part company. If you go to the left, I'll go to the right; if you go to the right, I'll go to the left."*

A Year of Prosperity

Abraham was so wealthy that the land could not hold all of his possessions...to the point that his servants and Lot's servants were fighting over the land! "What does that have to do with me?" you may ask. Well, Galatians 3 tells us that we have been adopted into the sonship of Abraham, and therefore we are partakers of his covenant *and* his blessing. And that blessing makes us rich!

> **Galatians 3:7, 13, 14 (KJV)**
> [7]Know ye therefore that they which are of faith, the same are the children of Abraham.
> [13]Christ hath redeemed us from the curse of the law, being made a curse for us: for it is written, Cursed is every one that hangeth on a tree:
> [14]That the **blessing of Abraham** might come on the Gentiles through Jesus Christ; that we might receive the promise of the Spirit through faith.

But even more important than being made rich is the fact that God adds no "sorrow" with our blessing. The word *sorrow* is translated from a Hebrew word that means *labor*. In other words, God blesses us with no strings attached.

What is rich? Rich is being able to drive a brand new Mercedes. What is sorrow? Sorrow is a $950 car payment every month. What is rich? Rich is having brand-new cherry furniture throughout your house. What is sorrow? Sorrow is paying on it for the next 36 to 48 months. Debt only *adds* labor to your purchases.

Many people live under the *illusion* of prosperity when they really live in bondage of debt. When God blesses you, you don't have to add labor to it—you don't have to work extra for it. I have heard Christians praise the Lord when they got approved for a brand new credit card. But credit is not the answer to their problems, the Blessing of the Lord is!

A Year of Prosperity

Trust God to meet all of your needs. And know that when *He* meets your needs, you won't have to add labor for them. You won't even have to go into debt to get it.

Chapter 24

More Than Enough

God has many names throughout the Bible. Some of His Names include Jehovah (Self-Existent Redeemer), Elohim (Supreme Magistrate), Prince of Peace, King of Kings, Lord of Lords, Jehovah-Jireh (Provider), Jehovah-Rohi (Shepherd), and Jehovah-Nissi (Banner of Victory)...just to name a *few*. These names describe His many attributes.

One name that He has is El Shaddai. It is commonly translated "God of More Than Enough." A more precise, although uncommon, translation is "Double-Breasted God" or "Many-Breasted God." The idea is that just as a mother has more than one source of nourishment for her nursing baby, God also has more than enough provision for us.

Psalm 23:5 shows us that God will fill our cup overflowing with excess. In Luke 5, when Jesus first met Peter, He blessed him with a good catch of fish. The catch was so big that in verse 6 we find that the net began to break. And in verse 7 we find that two ships began to sink because of the catch! In John 21, when Jesus again blessed Peter with a good catch of fish, the load was so great that they could not haul in the net. In Genesis 13, Abraham had so much blessing...so many possessions, that the land could not support it all.

I believe that the Almighty Creator of everything that ever was and ever will be probably knows how much a cup can hold before it starts to overflow. The Self-Existent Redeemer must certainly know how much a net can hold before it starts to

A Year of Prosperity

break. The God of the Universe surely knows how much a ship can hold before it starts to sink. The Omnipotent, Omnipresent, and Omniscient Lord God must know how much fish a net can hold before it becomes too heavy for men to haul it in. I would certainly think that God Almighty knows how many possessions a man can have before the land can no longer support him.

You see, God is not concerned about *wasting* His blessing. He has more than enough blessing to go around. It is not as though He is in danger of running out of supply. He most definitely does not mind blessing you with more—even much more than you need. In Malachi 3, He tells us that He will open up the windows of Heaven and pour out a blessing so large that we will not have room to contain it.

Having more than we need...more than we can contain makes it so much easier to bless others. It allows us to be "generous on every occasion" because He will supply "seed to the sower." (2 Corinthians 9:10, 11)

Having seed to sow means that we have received more than enough harvest, to the point that the excess can be used to sow yet again...receiving yet another harvest of *more than enough!* I once heard a preacher say, "If what you have is not big enough to be considered your harvest, make it your seed instead."

As you sow your seed in faith, don't ever be intimidated to believe God for a harvest of *more than enough.* He has no problem with giving it to you. He has done it many times for other people in the Bible, and He will do it for you.

Chapter 25

Redeemed From Moth and Rust

Genesis 3:16-19 (NIV)
[16] *To the woman he (God) said, "I will greatly increase your pains in childbearing; with pain you will give birth to children. Your desire will be for your husband, and he will rule over you."*
[17] *To Adam he said, "Because you listened to your wife and ate from the tree about which I commanded you, 'You must not eat of it,' "Cursed is the ground because of you; through painful toil you will eat of it all the days of your life.*
[18] *It will produce thorns and thistles for you, and you will eat the plants of the field.*
[19] *By the sweat of your brow you will eat your food until you return to the ground, since from it you were taken; for dust you are and to dust you will return."*

Matthew 6:19 (NIV)
[19] (Jesus said) *Do not store up for yourselves treasures on earth, where **moth and rust destroy**, and where thieves break in and steal.*

There is a curse manifesting on this planet. In Genesis, Adam was given dominion over the earth, which was a paradise at the time. But Adam sinned and a curse was brought into the earth. It was not God's Will for the curse to be allowed in the earth, but Adam's legal dominion over the

A Year of Prosperity

earth legally had to be turned over to Satan because of Adam's sin.

Because of that curse, men bring provision by the sweat of their brow, women must travail in child birth, and moth and rust corrupt our belongings. Cars rust and their tires wear out. Houses' roofs do not last forever. Clothing gets tattered after use. Televisions stop working after a while. Moth and rust destroy.

The Bible says in Galatians 3 that we have been redeemed from that curse! Christ became a curse so that we could live outside the curse. This means that every element of the curse can be annihilated by faith. Men do not have to work by the sweat of their brow; women do not have to travail in child birth; and moth and rust do not have to destroy our possessions.

When I was growing up, we had a microwave that quit working. It did not work for months. We tried everything to get it to work...we tried unplugging it and plugging it back in; we tried pushing all the buttons. Nothing worked! The microwave remained powerless. At the time, finances were tight and we did not have money for a new microwave. One night at the dinner table, Dad wanted to heat up his coffee but couldn't. Rather than get upset, he decided to have the whole family lay hands on the microwave. So my Dad, Mom, my two brothers and I laid hands on it and commanded it to come back on. Immediately, the microwave came back on, and it worked for *years* after that! Around the same time, our car started leaking coolant. Dad and I laid hands on the car and commanded the leak to stop. It stopped leaking immediately!

Moth and rust are costly! They cause items and possessions to wear out, forcing us to buy new ones. That is not an issue if money is abundant. But if money is still an issue for you, you can live above the curse by faith. Do not fall into condemnation because you don't have enough money to buy new possessions. By faith you can command your

A Year of Prosperity

possessions to last longer. Trust and believe God and claim His promise to redeem you from moth and rust!

Chapter 26

God is a God of Reward – Part 1

> **Hebrews 11:6 (KJV)**
> *But without faith it is impossible to please him: for he that cometh to God must believe that he is, and that he is a **rewarder** of them that diligently seek him.*

The first thing we must do is understand that God <u>is</u>—that He *exists*. Most Christians don't have a problem with that. But immediately after acknowledging that He exists, we must acknowledge that He is a rewarder. It is God's pleasure to bestow reward to His kids.

We saw in chapter 19 that when we sow our hurts, He rewards us. It is the character of a loving Father to bestow reward on His children.

> **Jesus said in Matthew 7:11 (NIV)**
> *If you, then, though you are evil, know how to give good gifts to your children, how much more will your Father in heaven give good gifts to those who ask him!*

As a father, I understand that I am the only picture of fatherhood that my kids will get. If I want my kids to correctly understand God's character as a rewarder, then I must be a rewarder.

The following is an example of one of the ways that I am teaching my children the concept of reward: I am a worship leader, songwriter and producer. At the time of this writing, I have produced 3 of my own CDs and many others for other artists. I have had several of my songs recorded by other artists, and some have had national and even international exposure. Every night before bed, my 4-year-old daughter says her prayers. On top of the several things that she prays for, she always asks God to "help Daddy sell more CDs and more songs."

Recently, I got an unexpected royalty check for a CD project of which I was not even aware. A Christian university picked up one of my songs and recorded it on their newest project. They only made a few thousand copies, but the royalty check was still nice.

My daughter was a part of that harvest. As a result, I sat her down and explained to her that her prayers allowed Daddy to make some extra money. I explained that Jesus blessed Daddy because of her prayers. Then I took her to the toy store and let her pick out a toy. After all, she has just as much right to partake of the reward as I do!

A friend of mine was in a store one day with his kids. His kids kept saying (as kids tend to do), "Daddy, Daddy, can I have a toy? Daddy, Daddy, can I have a toy?" Almost instinctively, my friend said (as parents tend to do), "NO!" Then the Spirit of God immediately spoke to him and said, "Why did you tell them no? What good thing do I withhold from you? How will they learn My character as a rewarder if you don't reward them?" As you may have guessed, his kids got a toy.

We will continue looking at the concept of reward in the next chapter.

Chapter **27**

<u>God is a God of Reward – Part 2</u>

There are those who teach that the only reward promised to Christians is the reward of Heaven. They say that prosperity is not part of our covenant. They say that healing is only promised to us in the afterlife. But God's Word clearly tells us that we have a right to good things here on earth, just as much as in Heaven.

> **Psalm 23:6 (KJV)**
> *Surely goodness and mercy shall follow me **all the days of my life**, and I will dwell in the house of the LORD forever.*

David shows us that because God is our shepherd, we have the right to live in goodness and mercy all of our life. Then, when this life is over, we will dwell with Him forever.

> **Mark 10:29, 30 (NIV)**
> [29] *"I tell you the truth," Jesus replied, "no one who has left home or brothers or sisters or mother or father or children or fields for me and the gospel*
> [30] *will fail to receive a hundred times as much **in this present age** (homes, brothers, sisters, mothers, children and fields–and with them, persecutions) and in the age to come, eternal life."*

Jesus tells us again that whatever we sacrifice for the gospel will be measured back to us "in this present age." Then, in the age to come, we can enjoy eternal life!

A Year of Prosperity

I have seen bumper stickers and T-shirts that say, "Work for God. The pay is not great, but the benefits are out of this world!" I don't agree with that sentiment. I believe that the pay *is* great – *and* the rewards are out of this world!

In chapter 19 of this book, we saw that when we sow our hurts, our "reward will be great" (Luke 6:35). God is a God of reward in the here and now, as well as in the eternal rewards of Heaven!

Someone once told me, "You can have Heaven on your way to Heaven, or you can have hell on your way to Heaven. It's up to you." We have the right to live above the curse in the earth, and to receive rewards when we diligently seek Him.

Chapter 28

<u>What is in Your Hand?</u>

In Exodus 4, Moses had an encounter with God. He was concerned about his upcoming meeting with Pharaoh because he thought people would not believe that He was sent from God. God asked Moses, "What is in your hand?" Moses showed God his staff. God told Moses to throw it on the ground. When he did, it turned into a snake. God told Moses to use this staff to show Pharaoh a miraculous sign from God.

In 1 Kings 17, Elijah met a widow during a time of famine. He was hungry, so he asked her if she had any bread and water. The widow was about to use her last bit of flour and oil to prepare a final meal for her and her son. Elijah asked her to make him a meal before she made one for herself and her son. She did so, and the Bible says her flour and oil did not run out for the rest of the famine.

In Matthew 14, Jesus had just finished preaching to a crowd of 5,000 people. They were hungry and had very little food. The disciples wanted Jesus to send the people into town so they could buy food. But Jesus asked them how much food they had. They told him that they had 5 loaves of bread and 2 fishes. He asked them to give the food to him. He blessed the food and it was miraculously multiplied to the point that it fed all 5,000 people, with 12 baskets of leftovers to spare!

These three stories all illustrate the same principle. If we can take what is in our hands and put it in God's Kingdom, He now has legal access to bless it. When He blesses it, He

A Year of Prosperity

multiplies it miraculously, meets our needs and blesses us with more than enough!

That is the whole principle behind the concept of tithing and offering. When we put 10% of our income into the Kingdom of God, He now has legal access to bless and multiply the other 90%. In other words, we put our finances in His Kingdom so that He can put His Kingdom in our finances!

> **This same principle is explained in Matthew 10:41 (NLT).** *If you welcome a prophet as one who speaks for God, you will receive the same reward a prophet gets.*

God showed Moses that if he gave God what was in his hand, God could bless it and use it miraculously. Elijah understood that if the widow could bless a man of God with what she had in her hand, God could multiply it and use it to supply her need. Jesus knew that if someone among the 5,000 could take something from their hands and put it in His hands, He could multiply it to bless them with what they needed.

What is in your hand? What can you put in the Kingdom of God so that God can put His Kingdom in you? What can you do for a man of God so that you can receive the same reward as that man of God?

You cannot give what you do not have. Because of this, I do not believe that Christians should put tithes and offerings on their credit cards. We should only give what is in our hands. But do not be intimidated to put what you have in God's hands. Your reward will be great. Your finances will be sanctified, multiplied, and protected. You will be blessed with all you need and even more than enough!

Chapter 29

Praise and Giving

As I have stated before I am a worship leader. I have been a full-time music minister since 1993. In my studies of praise, worship and music in the Bible, I have found that there is a relationship between praise and giving.

It may interest you to know that the very first instance of praise in the Bible is in the same verse as the very first instance of tithing. We find this in Genesis 14:20 when Melchizedek, the priest said, "And blessed be the most high God, which hath delivered thine enemies into thy hand. And he (Abraham) gave him tithes of all."

So right from the beginning, praise and tithes went together. But the relationship goes deeper than that.

Throughout the Bible we see that God wants His people to be self-controlled, patient and gentle (Galatians 5:22 & 23). He wants us to be sober, self-aware and alert (1 Peter 5:8). He expects our behavior to be moderate and reserved...or does He?

There are seven different Hebrew words that are translated *praise* in the Old Testament. The most common of those seven is the word *Halal*, which is where we get the word *Hallelujah*. It is found over 160 times in the Old Testament, 117 of which are translated *praise*. Its literal translation is *to be clamorously foolish and speak until you are beside yourself.*

A Year of Prosperity

Praise looks like foolishness to the world. It also looks like foolishness to the natural mind. But 1 Corinthians 1:27 tells us that God uses foolishness to confound the wise. Praise rarely looks like it makes sense.

It did not make sense for Paul and Silas to praise God while they were in prison (Acts 16); but they did and God freed them. It did not make sense for Israel to praise God rather than draw the sword against the advancing armies of Moab and Ammon (2 Chronicles 20); but they did, and God confused the armies, killing each other off...to the very last man! It did not make sense for David, King of Israel, to dance on dirty streets where he was usually carried on the shoulders of men (2 Samuel 6); but he did, and God called him a man after His own heart. (Acts 13:22)

Praise, like giving, moves the hand and the heart of God. If you are going through a struggling circumstance, give God praise that He is the answer to your problem. Praise Him that He has already met your need. Among its many benefits, your praise ushers God's presence (Psalm 22:3); it stills the attack of Satan (Psalm 8:2); and it destroys depression. (Isaiah 61:3)

In 2 Corinthians 9:7 we see that God "loves a cheerful giver." The word "cheerful" in this verse was translated from a Greek word that means *hilarious*. Isn't it interesting that God wants us to be sober and self-controlled until it comes to our praise and our giving? He wants us to be *clamorously foolish* praisers and *hilarious* givers!

Praise and giving have been working together since the very beginning. Whatever your particular need may be, mix your praise with your giving and watch the Hand of God move in your life!

Chapter **30**

<u>**Paying Your Taxes**</u>

In Matthew 22, Mark 12 and Luke 20 we see three different accounts of the same story. Jesus was asked if Christians were obligated to pay taxes. And it was here that Jesus said the often-quoted phrase, "Render unto Caesar that which is Caesar's, and render unto God that which is God's." In other words, Christians should pay their taxes.

In another story in Matthew 17, we find that Jesus helped Peter to pay his taxes by leading him to catch a fish. The fish contained a coin in its mouth that was worth enough to pay both Jesus' and Peter's taxes. So we see that God Himself will help us pay our taxes. But let us look at that story a little closer:

> **Matthew 17:24-27 (NIV)**
> [24] *After Jesus and his disciples arrived in Capernaum, the collectors of the two drachma tax came to Peter and asked, "Doesn't your teacher pay the temple tax?"*
> [25] *"Yes, he does," he replied.   When Peter came into the house, Jesus was the first to speak. "What do you think, Simon?" he asked. "From whom do the kings of the earth collect duty and taxes–from their own sons or from others?"*
> [26] *"From others," Peter answered.   "Then the sons are exempt," Jesus said to him.*
> [27] *"But so that we may not offend them, go to the lake and throw out your line. Take the first fish you catch; open its mouth and you will find a four drachma coin. Take it and give it to them for my tax and yours."*

A Year of Prosperity

Verse 24 says that this tax was a tax for God's temple. And of course, Jesus and Peter were both sons of God. Jesus explained that because He and Peter were both sons of God, they were exempt from this tax. But to avoid offending people, Jesus gave Peter instructions on how to get money to pay this tax. That's right...Jesus helped Peter pay a tax that HE DID NOT OWE!

There is a growing movement of people in the United States who are refusing to pay income taxes. They say that the federal income tax is illegal and fraudulent. Many have sued the IRS and have even won! In courts many people have proven, constitutionally, that the 16th Amendment (which established the income tax) was never properly ratified by the States, making it illegally imposed on the American people. Some Christians have joined this bandwagon, stating that they are not obligated to "render to Caesar" that which is *not* legally Caesar's.

My point of view is this. It does not matter that the 16th Amendment was never properly ratified. It does not matter if income tax is legal or illegal. If you walk in the abundance of God's commanded blessing, if you always have "more than enough," and if money is not an issue for you, what difference should income tax make (or any other tax, for that matter)? God helped Peter pay a tax that he did not owe...will He not do the same for us? If you truly operate in the abundance, provision and blessing of God, petty things like income taxes will not matter to you.

Do not jeopardize your witness and testimony as a Christian by failing to pay your taxes. Trust and believe God to do the same for you as He did for Peter. Be faithful in every area of your finances so as not to cut off the flow of God's blessing *to* your finances. Render unto Caesar that which is Caesar's whether you legally owe it or not. I believe this same principle can be applied to traffic tickets that you receive unjustly. God can and will bless you far beyond any tax or fine that you

A Year of Prosperity

pay—especially when you pay it for the sake of your witness as a child of God.

Chapter 31

Pass the Biscuits

> **John 16:23b & 24 (KJV)**
> *[23b]Verily, verily, I say unto you, Whatsoever ye shall **ask** the Father in my name, he will give it you.*
> *[24]Hitherto have ye **asked** nothing in my name: ask, and ye shall receive, that your joy may be full.*

Jesus told us that He wants us to ask God for things. He wants to fulfill our joy. It is His greatest desire to bless us and give us all things to enjoy.

His Word says in 1 Timothy 6:17, "Charge them that are rich in this world, that they be not highminded, nor trust in uncertain riches, but in the living God, who giveth us richly *all things to enjoy.*" So God wants to give us all things to enjoy, but He is waiting for us to ask Him. He wants us to exercise our faith and believe Him for whatever we need and whatever we want...all for our enjoyment!

So what does it mean to ask God? To answer that question we must understand the character of God. God is our Father, and as such we tend to compare Him to our earthly father. But have you ever asked your earthly father for something, and He told you "No"? Of course, we all have. But God's Word says that if we ask God, we WILL receive. He won't tell you "No." His promises are "Yes!" and "Amen!"

Many Christians tend to compare asking God for something to a teenager asking his earthly father for the keys to the car. The father may or may not give him the keys. But we need to view the word *ask* in a different way.

A Year of Prosperity

Picture a Thanksgiving meal...turkey, stuffing, mashed potatoes and gravy, green bean casserole, cranberry sauce, fruit salad and buttermilk biscuits. There are eight people sitting at the table, and the biscuits are at the other end of the table. You do not have any biscuits, but you want some. So what do you do? You *ask* someone to pass the biscuits. When you ask them to pass the biscuits, do you have any doubt that they will pass them? Of course you don't. But you will not receive the biscuits unless you ask for them.

When you ask God for something, don't view it like a teenager asking Daddy for the keys to the car. View it as though you were sitting at the table asking God to "pass the biscuits." You can have whatsoever you ask. God will richly give you all things to enjoy. All you have to do is ask. He won't tell you "No." He won't turn you away. God's greatest pleasure is to "pass the biscuits."

Chapter 32

Can Rich People Enter Heaven?

> **Matthew 19:23, 24 (NIV)**
> *23 Then Jesus said to his disciples, "I tell you the truth, it is hard for a rich man to enter the kingdom of heaven.*
> *24 Again I tell you, it is easier for a camel to go through the eye of a needle than for a rich man to enter the kingdom of God."*

There are several interpretations of the meaning of this passage. Some people have interpreted this passage to mean that it is impossible for rich people to enter heaven. But we know that it is possible, because Jesus said so in verse 26:

> *26 Jesus looked at them and said, "With man this is impossible, but with God all things are possible."*

One popular interpretation of verse 24 says that Jesus was referring to a small pedestrian gate in Jerusalem called the "Eye of the Needle", in which a camel could not pass unless he unloaded all of the baggage he was carrying. So the camel could pass if it was willing to let go of its belongings. The analogy is that only if a rich man was willing to let go of his wealth could he enter heaven.

This analogy would seem to be proven by Jesus' request that the young rich man go sell all of his possessions and give to the poor. However, many historians and Bible scholars are

A Year of Prosperity

now saying that there is no archaeological or historical proof of this gate called the "Eye of the Needle".

So what was Jesus saying? Obviously, economic status (or lack thereof) is not a prerequisite for salvation. We have already established time after time that there is a pattern in God's Word regarding prosperity. God does want us to be blessed, and yes, rich! Jesus was saying that we need to trust in God and not in riches in order to get to heaven. He was explaining that rich people tend to trust in riches, making it hard for them to receive salvation.

Only a few verses later, Jesus Himself said that whatever we leave for God's sake will be measured back to us one hundred fold in this lifetime. This means that we should not have any reservations about what we give for the sake of the Kingdom.

Paul said in 1 Timothy 6:17 (NIV)
[17] Charge them that are rich in this world, that they be not highminded, nor trust in uncertain riches, but in the living God, who giveth us richly all things to enjoy;

Paul explained that our trust should be in God alone. Rich people have a tendency to trust in money. Because of this, rich people would naturally have a hard time releasing their trust in money to put their trust in God. But it is definitely NOT impossible.

Your wealth should be a testimony of God's goodness and provision, not a hindrance to your salvation. What Christians need to remember is that we are always to seek God first and His righteousness. In the process, God will add unto us everything we have need of (Matthew 6).

Rich people can enter heaven, as long as their trust is in God. The basic idea here is that it is perfectly all right for you to

A Year of Prosperity

have money and things, as long as money and things don't have you.

Chapter 33

Do Rich People Worship Money?

There have been people who have said that God does not want us blessed or rich because rich people worship money. They have even said that God will not bless us because He will not bring anything into our lives that will take our focus off of Him. And in the last chapter, we saw that rich people do tend to trust in "uncertain" riches rather than God. This would seem to prove the point that rich people worship money...or would it?

I have had abundance, and I have had lack. So I speak from experience when I say this. It is not rich people that worship money, but rather it is poor people who worship money.

When you are poor, what are you constantly doing? You are constantly trying to figure out ways to get more money. It consumes your thoughts, dominates your conversation, rules your daily life and affects your decision-making processes. Poor people are always trying to find a way to pay the next bill, get out of debt, pay their overdue mortgage payment, pay their overdue car payment, etc.

What occupies your thought-life the most is the thing you worship. For poor people, it is typically the acquisition of funds that occupies their thoughts the most. This applies to some rich people, too. But just because a person is rich does not mean that they will worship money.

Christian prosperity is not based on the quest for wealth. It is based on the quest for God. Jesus explained in Matthew

A Year of Prosperity

6:32, 33 that "...the pagans run after all these things, and your heavenly Father knows that you need them. But seek first his kingdom and his righteousness, and all these things will be given to you as well." (NIV)

Jesus explained that unbelievers are on a quest for wealth and possessions. But then He told us that if we make God our priority...if we make God the focus of our worship, He will bless us.

When God prospers us, it is almost impossible for us to worship money. Because we understand that our prosperity comes as a result of balanced priorities, not from seeking money. It comes as a result of our focus of worship being in the right place...towards God, not towards acquisition.

In conclusion, let's realize that even though some rich people do worship money, they typically do not worship money like poor people do. More importantly, Christians that seek first God's Kingdom have it best because their focus is in the right place. And they are prosperous because of it. As I said in the last chapter, it is perfectly all right for you to have money and things, as long as money and things don't have you.

Chapter 34

Does Money Make People Evil?

1 Timothy 6:9, 10 (NIV)
[9] People who want to get rich fall into temptation and a trap and into many foolish and harmful desires that plunge men into ruin and destruction.
[10] For the love of money is a root of all kinds of evil. Some people, eager for money, have wandered from the faith and pierced themselves with many griefs.

Many people have interpreted this passage to mean that money makes people evil. We have already established that people who are prosperous by God do not worship money, for they know that the worship of money is not what brings their prosperity but rather the worship of God. But as some believe, does money really make people evil?

Money has the ability to magnify who a person already is. Consider what would happen if an alcoholic obtained a lot of money. What would he do with the money? He would buy alcohol. What would happen if a gambler came into money? He would gamble with it. What would a sexual deviant do if he came into money? Perhaps we should not go there.

Now consider what would happen if a giving person came into money. What would they do with it? They would now have the capacity to give even more. An alcoholic with money becomes a bigger alcoholic. A gambler with money becomes a bigger gambler. A sexual deviant with money

A Year of Prosperity

becomes a bigger sexual deviant. A giver with money becomes a bigger giver.

Money does not make people evil, it just magnifies who they are. You may say, "Well, I knew someone who came into money, and they just turned into a big jerk." To that, I would submit that they were a *little* jerk before they came into money. Then, money magnified who they were and they became a "big jerk."

It is because of this that I believe some Christians have not yet experienced God's prosperity in their lives. God knows that some of us have issues in our lives that need to be addressed. And He would not want those issues to be magnified in who we are today. Rather, He wants to mold us and make us into what *He* wants us to be.

This is yet another example of how seeking God and His Kingdom first will allow Him to channel blessings through our life. As the verse above states, God does not want us to seek money because we may wander from the faith. But if we seek Him first, we allow Him to craft us in His image. So the next time you are tempted to stray from the faith...the next time you are tempted to sin, just say to yourself, "No, I'd rather prosper!"

After God has crafted us in His image, after He has eliminated these issues in our life, and after He has molded us, He can financially prosper us. And after we begin prospering, God will not have to be concerned about that prosperity magnifying who we are because who we are will only magnify Him.

Chapter 35

<u>We Are God's Kids</u>

I have stated several times in this book that God wants to prosper us financially. There is a clear pattern in Scripture showing that God desires His children to be financially secure, never lacking. The Bible also shows us that He wants us to live in abundance, with more than enough supply. But why does He want to prosper us? One of the reasons is so simple, yet so hard for some people to grasp; simply put, it's because He loves us and desires good things for us.

God is good. James 1:17 tells us that He is the giver of "good" and "perfect" gifts. Jesus said in Matthew 7 that if earthly parents know how to give good gifts unto their children, how much more will God give good gifts to His children? We are his kids, and He desires good things for us.

In the Old Testament, God's people were referred to as the "Children of Israel." Israel was the name that God gave to Jacob after He established a covenant with Jacob. The name "Israel" was symbolic of that covenant. So we could say that the "Children of Israel" were the "Children of the Covenant."

Fast-forward to the New Testament where God calls us "Children of God" (Romans 8:16); "Children of Light" (Ephesians 5:8); and "Sons of God" (1 John 3:1,2). We are no longer just children of a *covenant,* we are now God's kids!

A few years ago my mother called me and told me that my younger brother had gotten in a little trouble. He was in high school at the time and the family had just moved from

A Year of Prosperity

Michigan to Iowa. One morning, Mom came downstairs to find that her cell phone was missing, her car keys were gone, some money had been taken from her purse, and her car was not in the driveway. On the kitchen table there was a note that said, "I'm sorry, Mom. I had to get away for a little while. I'm in Michigan." Without asking, my brother had taken Mom's car and went back to Michigan (three states away) to visit some friends!

The interesting point is that, even though my brother messed up, my mother did not call the police. Why? Because he is one of her kids! If *anyone else* had taken some money from her purse, taken her cell phone, and taken her car across 3 states, she would have called the cops immediately. Furthermore, when my brother came home the next day, he still had a place to eat at the table, he still got Christmas and birthday presents, and he still had a bed to sleep in. Anyone else would not have been so fortunate. But after all, he is one of her kids.

You are one of God's kids. Just because you mess up once in a while does not mean that God will not continue to provide for you. His grace and mercy are abundant. Just as you desire to give good gifts to your kids, God wants to give good gifts to His kids! As much as you desire to see joy in the face of your children, God desires it even more so for us!

Chapter 36

Blessed to be a Blessing

In the last chapter, we saw that God prospers us because we are His kids. Let's look at another reason that God wants to prosper us.

Galatians 3 tells us that we have been adopted into the sonship of Abraham by our faith in Jesus. It also tells us that "all nations will be blessed" through Abraham and his descendants. Deuteronomy 15:6 says that we are to lend to many nations and not borrow. Psalm 112:5 tells us that a "good man shows favor and lends." And 2 Corinthians 9:11 (NIV) tells us that we will be made "rich in every way" so that we can be "generous on every occasion." We are blessed to be a blessing.

> **James 4:3 (NIV)**
> *When you ask, you do not receive, because you ask with wrong motives, that you may spend what you get on your pleasures.*

God wants to bless us with good things to enjoy, including finances, and pleasures. But He also wants to make sure that our motives are pure. As Luke 12:48 says, to whom much is given, much is required. As prosperous people of God, we have a responsibility to bless others. 1 Timothy 6:18 says that rich people should be "rich in good works" and "ready to distribute."

I know of millionaires who never spend any money on anyone but themselves. I know of millionaires who only spend money on other millionaires in order to boast of their wealth.

A Year of Prosperity

Rich people—especially rich Christians—ought to use their money and influence to help people and to help make other Christians prosperous so that they can do the same.

Now, let's talk about lending for a moment. We have already established in chapter 19 that we are to lend without expecting a return. But does God have anything else to say regarding lending?

> **Deuteronomy 23:19, 20 (NIV)**
> [19] *Do not charge your brother interest, whether on money or food or anything else that may earn interest.*
> [20] *You may charge a foreigner interest, but not a brother Israelite, so that the LORD your God may bless you in everything you put your hand to in the land you are entering to possess.*

The principle in this passage is that God's people are not to charge interest to God's people. We may charge interest to those outside our covenant (unbelievers), but we are supposed to lend to our Christian brothers without interest and even without expecting return! Debt puts others in bondage, and God does not want us to put our fellow brothers in bondage! We are blessed to be a blessing, not a curse.

We are to lend to the world, not the other way around! And I also believe that lending with interest is one of the ways that the wealth of the sinner is laid up for the just. (Proverbs 13:22)

Chapter 37

The Gospel to the Poor

In Luke 4:18, Scripture records Jesus going into the temple on the Sabbath. He opened the book of Isaiah, and turned to what we now refer to as (Isaiah) chapter 61, and began to read:

> ^{18} *The Spirit of the Lord is upon me, because he hath anointed me to preach **the gospel to the poor**; he hath sent me to heal the brokenhearted, to preach deliverance to the captives, and recovering of sight to the blind, to set at liberty them that are bruised,*
> ^{19} *To preach the acceptable year of the Lord.*

The very first purpose of the anointing that Jesus states is to "preach the gospel to the poor." The word *gospel* means *good news*. Jesus was saying that God anointed him to preach *good news* to the poor. So what is the good news to a poor person? The good news is that they do not have to be poor anymore!

For years, many Christians have been taught that God wants to keep us poor in order to keep us humble. But economic status has no bearing on humility. Some of the most stuck-up, loud-mouthed, conceited people I have ever met were poor people. The *good news* is that poverty does not make you humble.

For years, many Christians have been taught that money is the root of all evil. But the Bible actually says that it is the "love of money" that is "the root of all kinds of evil." The

A Year of Prosperity

"good news" is that, as Ecclesiastes 10:19 says, "money answers all things."

Just as Christians have been deceived that poverty equals humility, many Christians have also been taught that God wants to keep us poor in order to keep us from worshipping money. But, as we saw in chapter 33, it is poor people that worship money...not the rich. The *good news* is that if we worship God and put Him first, He will prosper us.

Perhaps sinking deeper into deception, Christians have been taught that money makes people evil. But, as we saw in chapter 34, money only magnifies who we are. The *good news* is that God wants to channel blessings to us as long as our magnification results in *His* magnification!

In Luke 7:23, Jesus told some followers of John the Baptist that "...the blind see, the lame walk, the lepers are cleansed, the deaf hear, the dead are raised, to the poor the gospel is preached."

Notice that the blind, the lame, the lepers, the deaf, and the dead got their immediate miracle. But the poor heard the *good news*. This is because godly prosperity is a result of a growth process based on our application of God's Word to our life. God will not just dump prosperity in our lap. But the *good news* is that if we apply His Word to our lives and our finances, we do not have to be poor!

Chapter 38

Our Daily Bread

In Matthew 6, Jesus gave us an example of how we ought to pray. In verse 11, he tells us to ask God to "Give us this day our daily bread."

In Exodus 16, we find that God fed the Children of Israel with daily manna. The manna was only good for the day it was given. By the next day, it would be rotten and filled with worms.

In 2 Corinthians 6, Paul tells us that today is the day of salvation. And in Matthew 6:34, Jesus tells us to take no thought for tomorrow, for tomorrow already has enough issues to worry about. As the old saying goes, "Tomorrow is promised to no man." The principle in these passages is that God provides for us on a day-to-day basis. He provided for the children of Israel on a daily basis, and He gives us our "daily" bread.

This is why debt is such a bad institution. Debt allows us to have something today, but it charges us tomorrow's provision. As Jesus said, tomorrow already has enough problems of its own to worry about. But debt forces us to add more issues to tomorrow's problems.

God promises to provide for us on a daily basis. We need not believe God for tomorrow's provision, just today's. If we trust Him to meet today's needs, we will not need to go into debt and steal from tomorrow's provision.

A Year of Prosperity

Consider how much you will end up paying for something if you buy it on credit. A $150,000 house on a 30-year mortgage at 7.5% interest will cost you over $375,000 over the life of the loan. The house will end up costing over 2 ½ times its value. The interest alone is over 150% of the appraised value of the house. A $20,000 car on a 5 year note at 7.5% interest will cost you over $24,000. This is a huge amount of tomorrow's provision already being spent and/or assigned—years before the money is actually made!

> **Proverbs 10:22 (KJV)**
> *The blessing of the LORD, it maketh rich, and he addeth no sorrow with it.*

The word "sorrow" in this verse means *labor*. By going into debt, you only add extra labor to your purchases. In the case of the house, you are adding over $225,000 worth of labor! God can bless you to the point that you do not have to add labor in order to obtain your blessing.

Keep in mind that you paid $150,000 for the house because that was what the house was worth *to you*. Perhaps you even haggled over the price a bit. You would never have agreed to a $375,000 purchase price for the house because the house was *only worth $150,000*. But debt forces you to pay *more* than the price *you* agreed on!

God is our provider. If you are in debt, it is very likely that you have trusted in debt to meet your need, rather than trusting in God's provision. If so, repent of relying on debt instead of relying on God. Then ask God to show you how to speed up the process of becoming debt-free! You can do it, and God will help you!

It is only after we are debt-free that we can start our journey toward true financial prosperity. And only after we are debt-free can we truly start trusting God for our *daily bread*. Daily bread is much less expensive than tomorrow's bread.

Chapter 39

Practical Principles Concerning Debt

Genesis 29 records that Jacob met Rachel and fell in love with her. He was willing to work for Laban, her father, for seven years in order to have Rachel. In a sense, this was like going into debt for seven years to receive what he wanted. Because of this biblical example, I think we can use this as a principle for our own finances: Do not get yourself into any kind of debt that you cannot get yourself out of in seven years. This is easier than you may think if you are fiscally responsible and do not make impulsive decisions and purchases.

If you are in debt and want to pay your debt off quickly, consider this method. When you open a new loan, make sure you get an amortization schedule from your lender. You will find that, at the beginning of the loan, the vast majority of your payment goes to interest only. Throughout the course of the loan, the percentages will change until, at the end of the loan, the vast majority of the payment will go to principal. The payment itself never changes, but the amounts allocated to interest and principal will.

With this in mind, find out how much of your payment is going to interest and how much is going to principal. For example, at the beginning of a mortgage, perhaps 90% is going to interest. So if you have a $1000 per month payment, $900 is going to interest.

A Year of Prosperity

During your first month, pay your $1000 payment. Then, using a separate check, pay an additional amount that covers the *principal only* for the second month's payment (probably around $100). Write "principal only" in the memo of the second check. You have just paid about $1100 and covered the principal for the first two months of your loan; plus you have saved $900.

During your second month, remember that you have already covered the principal for that month's payment. So, make your $1000 payment as usual, keeping in mind that your payment is actually covering the principal for the *third* month's payment, even though you are only in the second month of the loan. Then, write out a separate check for the principal for month 4 (perhaps $100 to $105 or so by this time). Make sure you do not forget to write "principal only" in the memo of that check.

You are now two months into your loan, and you have covered the principal for four months worth of payments, saving yourself almost $1800 in only two months! What would have taken you four months and cost $4000, has only taken you two months and about $2200.

If you keep this process up, you will cut your loan time in half, saving tens of thousands of dollars in the process. Keep in mind that your extra principal check will grow over the life of the loan, but the sacrifice will be more than worth it!

As a general rule, it is not a good idea to go into debt for items that will not appreciate or pay for themselves. Real estate appreciates. Cars do not. Furniture does not. Christmas presents do not. Vacations do not. An education does not appreciate, but it will more than pay for itself in the long run by allowing you to have a better paying job.

Of course, if you need a car in order to work, then buy a car. But DO NOT buy a new car! New cars depreciate on the order of 40% the moment they are driven off the lot. Also, stay

A Year of Prosperity

away from leases. They hardly make any financial sense. Being responsible today will assure a prosperous tomorrow. Let your prosperous tomorrows pay for new cars, fine furniture, and exotic vacations. This requires patience, and wouldn't you rather be free?

Chapter 40

<u>God Wants to Meet All of Your Needs</u>

As mentioned in chapter 24, one of God's many names in the Bible is _Jehovah-Jireh_, which means _the Lord provides._ Often in Scripture we see that God wants to provide our needs for us. Consider these Scriptures:

Philippians 4:19 (KJV)
But my God shall supply all your need according to his riches in glory by Christ Jesus.

Psalm 23:1 (NIV)
The LORD is my shepherd, I shall not be in want.

Matthew 6:7, 8 (NIV)
[7] And when you pray, do not keep on babbling like pagans, for they think they will be heard because of their many words.
[8] Do not be like them, for your Father knows what you need before you ask him.

Matthew 6: 31, 32 (NIV)
[31] So do not worry, saying, 'What shall we eat?' or 'What shall we drink?' or 'What shall we wear?'
[32] For the pagans run after all these things, and your heavenly Father knows that you need them.

A Year of Prosperity

These passages pretty well establish that God wants to meet our needs. But what is a need? Jesus addresses the obvious things like food, drink and clothing. Of course, shelter is also a need. But what other needs are there?

Our society is a little different than in Jesus' day. In this day and age, transportation is a need. In most instances, you cannot get a good job without a good car or without some other reliable means of daily transportation. Electricity is also a need. It provides light, heat, air conditioning, power for refrigerators, ovens, etc. Communication is also a necessity in today's society. We need to be able to talk to people, either by phone, email, cellular, etc.

With this in mind, do not be intimidated to ask God to supply these things for you. These are legitimate needs, and God is a need-meeter.

Consider one other interesting thing Jesus says in Matthew 6:

> **Matthew 6:26 (NIV)**
> *Look at the birds of the air; they do not sow or reap or store away in barns, and yet your heavenly Father feeds them. Are you not much more valuable than they?*

Jesus was saying that birds do not have the privilege of participating in the law of sowing and reaping, yet God still provides for them. How much more will God provide for us when we put sowing and reaping to work in our lives? Trust God when you sow, and He will meet all of your needs according to His riches!

Chapter 41

God Wants to Meet All of Your Wants

Most Christians will agree that God wants to meet all of our needs. In many cases, that type of theology crosses many denominational and doctrinal boundaries. However, it is sometimes very hard to convince Christians that God also wants to meet our wants. They believe that God is not touched by our wants, and that He does not care about them. This kind of theology is poor and does not paint an accurate picture of God's character. Even though it is popular theology, it is inaccurate. Let's look at a pattern in Scripture:

> **Psalm 37:4 (NIV)**
> *Delight yourself in the LORD and he will give you the **desires** of your heart.*

> **Psalm 103:2, 5 (NIV)**
> *[2] Praise the LORD , O my soul, and forget not all his **benefits**... [5] Who **satisfies your desires with good things** so that your youth is renewed like the eagle's.*

> **Mark 11:24 (KJV)**
> *Therefore I say unto you, What things **soever ye desire**, when ye pray, believe that ye receive them, and ye shall have them.*

A Year of Prosperity

> **1 Timothy 6:17 (KJV)**
> *Charge them that are rich in this world, that they be not highminded, nor trust in uncertain riches, but in the living God, who **giveth us richly all things to enjoy;***

> **John 16:24 (KJV):**
> *Hitherto have ye asked nothing in my name: ask, and ye shall receive, **that your joy may be full.***

> **James 1:17 (NIV)**
> *Every **good and perfect gift** is from above, coming down from the Father of the heavenly lights, who does not change like shifting shadows.*

God sees no problem in providing your wants as well as your needs. As we have covered earlier in this book, you are one of His kids, and He desires good things for His kids. We are perfectly welcome to have things, as long as things don't have us! As long as we are seeking God first, He desires to bless us with anything we ask!

I have known Christians to believe God for some of the most (seemingly) *ridiculous* things...ridiculous to some people, but not ridiculous to God. I know a Christian who believes God for a deer when he goes hunting, and he has gotten his deer every year for the past 18 years, usually in under 45 minutes! I know a Christian who asked God to help her find a lost earring, and God showed her where the earring was.

I believed God for a specific make and model of car and supernaturally received the car about 4 months later – for almost 30% below sticker. My wife asked and believed God for a brand new, maroon Chevy Venture Warner Brothers Edition minivan. She was very specific for what she asked

A Year of Prosperity

God to provide. And only three months later, she got one...exactly as she had asked...for over 45% off of the sticker price! What does God care if we have these things?

I know a Christian who once went deep-sea fishing off the coast of Hawaii. He had prayed and asked God for a Blue Marlin. The captain of the boat told him that Blue Marlins were not in that area during that season. The entire crew of the boat assured him that they would see no Blue Marlins that day. Later that afternoon, he caught a Blue Marlin. The captain and crew were hysterical! They knew that it was a miracle that this Christian man had caught a Blue Marlin.

Do not be intimidated to believe God for what you want. As long as your priorities are in check, He does not mind giving you the desires of your heart.

Chapter 42

<u>Prosperity Flows Out of Marriage Part 1</u>

Many Christians are very familiar with Malachi 3—the chapter that talks about tithing and offering. But it may interest you to know that in Malachi 2, God addresses some other important issues before He ever talks about tithing and offering.

> **Malachi 2:13-16 (NIV)**
> [13] *Another thing you do: You flood the LORD's altar with tears. You weep and wail because he no longer pays attention to your offerings or accepts them with pleasure from your hands.*
> [14] *You ask, "Why?" It is because the LORD is acting as the witness between you and the wife of your youth, because you have broken faith with her, though she is your partner, the wife of your marriage covenant.*
> [15] *Has not the LORD made them one? In flesh and spirit they are his. And why one? Because he was seeking godly offspring. So guard yourself in your spirit, and do not break faith with the wife of your youth.*
> [16] *"I hate divorce," says the LORD God of Israel, "and I hate a man's covering himself with violence as well as with his garment," says the LORD Almighty. So guard yourself in your spirit, and do not break faith.*

God was saying that Israel's prayers went unanswered and their offerings unaccepted because men did not have right

A Year of Prosperity

relationships with their wives. So then, prosperity flows out of marriage.

It was only after God addressed the marriage issue that He began to address tithing and offering. God was telling His people that He wanted to open the windows of Heaven and pour out a blessing too large to contain. But that would only happen after men restored right relationships with their wives. As you can see in Malachi 2:13, your tears, wailings and offerings mean nothing to God if your marriage is in shambles.

The words "broken faith" in verse 14 come from the Hebrew word *bagad*, which basically means, *to be unfaithful*. Being unfaithful does not necessarily mean committing the "act" of adultery because Jesus said, "...whosoever looketh on a woman to lust after her hath committed adultery with her already in his heart." (Matthew 5:28)

Get your marriage on the right track. That really should be the first step taken toward financial prosperity. And know that Satan will do anything he can to stop you from having a healthy marriage. Marriage is powerful! I truly believe that there is no prayer that is more powerful than the prayer of agreement between husband and wife. And I can personally testify that Louise and I have a 100% success rate when it comes to the prayer of agreement!

There is nothing out there that is worth sacrificing your marriage. In other words, there is nothing as valuable as your marriage. Satan knows this, and that is why he hates marriage. But as much as Satan hates marriage, God hates divorce even more. He knows that prosperity and success flow out of marriage. We will delve into this concept a little deeper in the next chapter.

Chapter 43

Prosperity Flows Out of Marriage Part 2

As I said in the previous chapter, I believe there is nothing more powerful than the prayer of agreement between husband and wife. Because of this, much success can be determined by the health and strength of a Christian marriage. Let's look at some principles regarding prosperity and marriage.

1) <u>Marriage and Money Are Intertwined</u>
We have already established that prosperity flows out of marriage. But it is interesting to note that as much as 80% of the arguments in marriage are money-related. Money becomes a subject that drives couples apart, when it should be doing the opposite. Couples should be coming together and praying in agreement over their finances; this will bring them success. Unfortunately, this is a concept that is quite foreign to many Christian couples.

2) <u>The Two Must Become One</u>
Amos 3:3 asks the question "Can two walk together, except they be agreed?" Malachi 2:15 says that the Lord has made the husband and wife "one." Jesus also addressed this issue in Matthew 19:4-6, when He said that God has made the husband and wife "one flesh," and that they are "joined together."

A Year of Prosperity

Because the husband and wife are supposed to be "one," I believe that it is unhealthy for husbands and wives to have separate bank accounts. We are supposed to be one in every aspect of our life and marriage. But if we are not one in our finances, how can we expect God to bless us financially?

James 1:7, 8 (NIV)
[7] That man should not think he will receive anything from the Lord;
[8] he is a doubleminded man, unstable in all he does.

If a double-minded man should not expect to receive anything from God, how can a double-minded marriage expect to receive from Him?

When Louise and I were first married, we had separate checking accounts, separate savings accounts, and separate bills. I am ashamed to say that I brought $15,000 worth of debt into our marriage. I did not tell this to Louise because of that shame. So I paid my bills from my accounts, and we kept our finances separate.

But later we realized that we needed to be one. So I lowered my pride enough to tell Louise about my debt. I closed my bank accounts, and Louise added me to hers. Then, we worked together to pay off my debt. We paid it off in less than a year and a half. How? By the Power of Agreement!

3) <u>A Man's Wife is His Wisdom</u>
It is interesting to note that *wisdom* in the Bible is most often referred to in the feminine sense. For example:

Proverbs 4:6 (NIV)
*Do not forsake wisdom, and **she** will protect you; love **her**, and **she** will watch over you.*

A Year of Prosperity

> **Proverbs 8:11 (NIV)**
> *For wisdom is more precious than rubies, and nothing you desire can compare with **her**.*

Your wife is your wisdom. This is why Proverbs 18:22 says that finding a wife is a "good thing" and that it brings God's favor. Proverbs 31:10 says that a virtuous woman is worth far more than rubies. And Proverbs 31:26 says that wisdom flows out of her mouth. Your wife is worth more than rubies because her wisdom will bring you prosperity and favor! So listen to what your wife has to say.

4) <u>Provision Comes Through the Husband</u>

I will be blunt and to the point. Husbands, your wives were not designed to carry the load of provider for the family. Two-income homes are destroying the American family. The wife should not be shouldering the burden, for it is not hers to carry.

I am not saying that it is wrong for a woman to work. Some women get fulfillment from their careers. And even Proverbs 31 says that a Godly woman makes money in the marketplace. But let's face it: a husband who *makes* his wife work typically does so because he does not have the faith to believe that God can supply everything the family needs through him.

At the time that Louise and I came to this revelation, it could have been a difficult decision for me to have her quit her career. But we both knew that it was the right and Godly thing for us to do so that our house would be in order. And even though she was making over $90,000 a year, we did not hesitate in our decision for her to come home and take her rightful place in mothering our children.

A Year of Prosperity

God immediately started showering me abundantly with blessings and open doors after we made that decision...not the least of which was my first internationally distributed song, recorded by the world's largest praise and worship record label.

Men, it is up to us to ensure that our marriages are strong and healthy. It is up to us, the priests of our homes, to initiate prayer times with our wives. It is up to us to be the providers in our homes. We need to work together to allow God to prosper our families. Husbands, the buck stops with us! Let's work on strengthening our marriage covenants so that prosperity and success can flow freely.

Chapter 44

Money Answers All Things

> **Ecclesiastes 10:19 (NIV)**
> *A feast is made for laughter, and wine makes life merry, but **money is the answer for everything**.*

The King James version of this verse says that "money answereth all things," meaning that money is not just the answer, but that it does the answering. There is an old saying that says "Money talks." Apparently money *does* talk—because it answers! What does it answer? Everything!

What issues do you have in life that need to be *answered*? We have already stated that 80% of arguments in marriage are money-related. And over 50% of marriages in the U.S. end in divorce. Among some minorities, that number is well over 60%. Unfortunately, the statistics do not change much among Christians. With those numbers in mind, I am forced to wonder how many marriages could have been saved if it were not for increasing financial tensions burdening the marriage as a whole. How many of those marriages had issues that were *talking*, but had no money to do the *answering*?

Here are some examples of issues that *talk* to us in some of life's everyday circumstances:

- "If only the kids didn't need braces this year, we could have gone on a family vacation..."
- "If only we could afford a private school, the kids wouldn't have to deal with so many social problems..."

A Year of Prosperity

- "If only the house didn't need a new roof, we could have had a nicer Christmas…"
- "If only the grandparents didn't live so far away, the family could visit more often…"
- "If only the wife and I could get away for a few days, we could rekindle our relationship…"
- "If only I could take some time off work, I would have more time to spend with the kids…" or "If only I didn't have to work, I could home-school my children."
- "If only I didn't need the overtime…"
- "If only I didn't have to travel so much…"
- "If only our church could finish this building project…"
- "If only dad would have had insurance…"

And the list goes on and on. These are all things that money could fix. How many issues do we face in life that would be eradicated if we simply had the money to *answer* the problem?

Not long ago, I moved my family into a new home in a different state. We were on a time crunch due to the scheduled closing of our previous home. The family that was living in our new home had to be out of the house within two weeks. This was extremely difficult for them. In fact, they had to cancel their family vacation in order to be out of their house on time…all because of *our* tight time schedule.

On the day of the move, they were not yet completely out of our (new) house. So we were moving in at the same time that they were moving out. I could tell that they were stressed and perhaps even a little perturbed with us. A week or so later, I ran into them at a very nice restaurant. As I left the restaurant, I approached their server privately and told her that I wanted to buy their dinner. The server arranged for it, and I paid their check and left.

A few days later I was told that they were greatly touched by that act of kindness. As you can see, money was able to

A Year of Prosperity

answer what might have been an otherwise tense situation between us.

What would you do if money were not an issue in your life? How would you live? What would you drive? Who or what would you sow into? What would you do for your family? For your friends? For those less fortunate? For the gospel? For your local church?

Money is not supposed to be an issue for a believer. Our covenant was established so that we could live in victory in every area of our life. This includes our finances! If we can live in the overflow of God's provision, many problems will be *answered.* Trust and believe God for the money to answer <u>ALL</u> things<u>.</u> Then receive it gladly when it comes, for it is His good pleasure to channel blessing, provision, and abundance into your life.

Chapter 45

Uncap Your Potential!

In Genesis 29, Jacob made an agreement with Laban to work for seven years in order to receive Laban's daughter Rachel for his wife. Verse 20 says that the seven years seemed like only days to Jacob because he loved Rachel so much. But at the end of those seven years, Laban cheated Jacob and gave him his other daughter Leah instead.

Jacob was angry with Laban for deceiving him, yet he agreed to work for Laban for another seven years in order to receive Rachel—the one he truly loved. By the end of the next seven years, Laban had become a very prosperous man. And this was all because of Jacob's hard work.

By Genesis 30:25, Jacob had fulfilled his obligation to Laban and wanted to return to his homeland with his wives. Laban recognized that he was prosperous only because of God's blessing on Jacob's hard work, so he did not want to let Jacob go. Nevertheless, Laban told Jacob that he could leave, and that all he had to do was name his wages. But Jacob did not trust Laban because Laban had deceived him.

This brings us up to Genesis 30:29-33 (NIV)

29 Jacob said to him (Laban), "You know how I have worked for you and how your livestock has fared under my care.
30 The little you had before I came has increased greatly, and the LORD has blessed you wherever I have been. But now, when may I do something for my own household?"

A Year of Prosperity

> *[31] "What shall I give you?" he asked. "Don't give me anything," Jacob replied. "But if you will do this one thing for me, I will go on tending your flocks and watching over them:*
> *[32] Let me go through all your flocks today and remove from them every speckled or spotted sheep, every dark-colored lamb and every spotted or speckled goat. They will be my wages.*
> *[33] And my honesty will testify for me in the future, whenever you check on the wages you have paid me. Any goat in my possession that is not speckled or spotted, or any lamb that is not dark-colored, will be considered stolen."*

We've already learned that Laban had cheated Jacob by turning a 7-year contract into a 14-year contract. And in Genesis 31:7, Jacob tells Rachel and Leah that Laban had cheated him on his wages 10 times! More importantly, Jacob knew that *wages* represented a capped potential, so rather than receive wages from Laban and risk being cheated again, Jacob decided to start his own business. He knew how to tend flocks, for by now he had been doing that for years. And all this time, he watched another man grow prosperous from his efforts, knowing all the while that it was the blessing of the Lord on *himself* that granted prosperity to Laban.

If you want to receive prosperity in your life, I strongly suggest that you *uncap your potential*. Hourly wages and salaries represent capped potential. Wages and salaries do not offer more money for more work, nor do they offer more money for better work. I suggest finding a job that grants more money for more and better work.

Commissioned sales is a perfect example of this. The more you sell, the more you make, thereby uncapping your potential. Owning your own business is another example of this. The more you can put into the business, the more you can get out of the business. I realize this is a step of faith. But uncapping your potential can mean the difference between just getting by and stepping into overflow. If you are

A Year of Prosperity

intimidated to leave your job and start your own business, you may consider starting a part-time business on the side.

Success in business requires training and discipline and hard work. But if you're not frightened by these things, the opportunities are just as great today as they ever were. – **David Rockefeller**

More on this idea in the next chapter...

Chapter 46

God Ideas

Let us look a little closer at Jacob's business venture. We will see that God gave Jacob some very specific business ideas to ensure his success. Jacob had agreed with Laban to take all of Laban's spotted, speckled, and dark-haired sheep and goats. And again, Laban tried to cheat Jacob (as he had done many times before) by removing all the blemished animals from his flocks. But God showed Jacob how to "stack the deck" in his own favor:

> **Genesis 30:37-43 (NIV)**
> [37] *Jacob, however, took fresh-cut branches from poplar, almond and plane trees and made white stripes on them by peeling the bark and exposing the white inner wood of the branches.*
> [38] *Then he placed the peeled branches in all the watering troughs, so that they would be directly in front of the flocks when they came to drink. When the flocks were in heat and came to drink,*
> [39] *they mated in front of the branches. And they bore young that were streaked or speckled or spotted.*
> [40] *Jacob set apart the young of the flock by themselves, but made the rest face the streaked and dark-colored animals that belonged to Laban. Thus he made separate flocks for himself and did not put them with Laban's animals.*
> [41] *Whenever the stronger females were in heat, Jacob would place the branches in the troughs in front of the animals so they would mate near the branches,*

A Year of Prosperity

> ^{42} *but if the animals were weak, he would not place them there. So the weak animals went to Laban and the strong ones to Jacob.*
> ^{43} *In this way the man grew exceedingly prosperous and came to own large flocks, and maidservants and menservants, and camels and donkeys.*

We see here that Jacob was selectively breeding his own streaked, speckled and spotted sheep by tainting their water supply. He was also allowing the weaker sheep to breed unblemished in order to breed the stronger ones for himself. This may seem crooked, but in Genesis 31:10-12 we see that the Lord Himself showed Jacob in a dream how to do this:

> ^{10} *"In breeding season I once had a dream in which I looked up and saw that the male goats mating with the flock were streaked, speckled or spotted.*
> ^{11} *The angel of God said to me in the dream, 'Jacob.' I answered, 'Here I am.'*
> ^{12} *And he said, 'Look up and see that all the male goats mating with the flock are streaked, speckled or spotted, for I have seen all that Laban has been doing to you.*

God showed Jacob how to start his own business and how to prosper from someone who had been cheating him for years. You may wonder why God would have shown Jacob how to *cheat* someone out of his business. It is because God does not have any obligation toward those who are not in covenant with Him. Laban was a Syrian who had no relationship with God. God's whole purpose in sending Jacob to Laban was so that Jacob could leave with Laban's daughters and his prosperity. Laban's wealth was laid up for Jacob (Proverbs 13:22) and God showed Jacob how to get it.

Just as God showed Jacob how to prosper, and showed Peter how to pay his taxes by catching a fish, He will give us

A Year of Prosperity

God ideas for uncapping our potential and bringing prosperity into our lives! Realize, though, that a *good* idea is not always a *God* idea. In 1 Chronicles 17, King David told Nathan the priest that he thought it was time to build God a temple. David did not believe that it was fair for him to live in a cedar palace while the Ark of the Covenant rested in a tent. Nathan told David to go ahead and do whatever he had in mind. Then God corrected Nathan and told him that is was not His desire that David build Him a temple. It was a good idea, but not a *God* idea.

Statistics have shown that the average person receives 27 ideas in their lifetime that would make them a millionaire, if they would only follow through with their idea. It is not enough for God to give us ideas to prosper us; we must put the ideas to work. This requires faith, patience and persistence. It also requires a keen ear to the voice of God as He leads us every step of the way.

Remember too that God ideas do not always make sense to the natural mind. Peter, a professional fisherman, most likely thought that Jesus' idea of catching a fish with a coin in its mouth was ridiculous. You may think your business idea is ridiculous, but keep in mind that people have made millions of dollars selling such "ridiculous" items as Pet Rocks, Chia Pets, and bottled water! Some thought they were ridiculous ideas, while others acted on the ideas and now laugh all the way to the bank.

In the modern world of business, it is useless to be a creative original thinker unless you can also sell what you create. Management cannot be expected to recognize a good idea unless it is presented to them by a good salesman. **– David M. Ogilvy**

Pray and ask God to give you a *God* idea that will uncap your potential and channel true prosperity into your life. Then, get to work, knowing that whatever your hands touch will prosper! (Deuteronomy 28:12)

Chapter 47

The Covenant of Faith
Part 1: What Faith Is

We are going to spend the next five chapters studying the concept of faith because the believer's prosperity is never going to come without faith. I want you to study these chapters very closely and carefully, for the whole principle of prosperity operates by faith. Get these concepts in your spirit. Your success depends on it.

Our covenant is a covenant based on faith. In the Old Testament, their covenant was based on sacrifices, offerings, penance and works. But under the New Covenant, our salvation is based on God's grace and our faith—not works!

> **Ephesians 2:8, 9 (NIV)**
> [8] *For it is by grace you have been saved, through faith–and this not from yourselves, it is the gift of God–*
> [9] *not by works, so that no one can boast.*

Everything we receive under the New Covenant is received the same way—by grace through faith. Salvation, healing, deliverance, provision, prosperity...they are all received by grace through faith. So it now becomes necessary to define our terms. What is grace, and what is faith?

Simply defined, grace is *God's ability.* It is not by our ability that we are saved, but by God's ability. Our works don't grant us salvation, but rather God's works from 2000 years ago. If

A Year of Prosperity

our ability would grant us salvation, we would have the opportunity to boast, but God refuses to share His glory with anyone.

Faith is defined in Hebrews 11:1 (NIV)
Now faith is being sure of what we hope for and certain of what we do not see.

Faith can be defined as *confident expectation*. We can be confidently expectant when we pray and ask God for the things we need or want, based on His Word. Faith is <u>always</u> based on the Word of God, and <u>His Word only</u>.

Romans 10:17 (KJV)
So then faith cometh by hearing, and hearing by the word of God.

Faith ultimately comes from the Word of God. His Word spells out everything that is available in our covenant. We know that God is always true, never false. So when we see a promise in His Word, we know that we can receive it with *confident expectation*. We can be "sure of what we hope for and certain of what we do not see."

Throughout this entire book we have established the fact that God wants us to be financially prosperous; we need not doubt this. God's Word assures us that prosperity is available to us. But as it is with every other element of our covenant, we will only receive it when we exercise our faith for it.

Faith is knowing what God's Word says then putting it into practice and receiving His promises. If we truly know and believe God's Word, it shouldn't be hard to receive those promises, "for no matter how many promises God has made, they are 'Yes' in Christ. And so through him the 'Amen' is spoken by us to the glory of God."
(2 Corinthians 1:20 - NIV)

A Year of Prosperity

When I was a child, I was taught that when we pray, God will give us one of three answers. He will either say "Yes!", "No!", or "Wait!" But now I know assuredly that when it comes to His promises, His answer is always "Yes!" and always "Amen!" These promises include salvation, healing, deliverance, strength, joy, provision...and "Yes," prosperity!

Chapter **48**

The Covenant of Faith
Part 2: What Faith Is *Not*

Last chapter we talked a little about what faith is, but now we'll look at what faith is *not*.

<u>Faith Is Not Hope</u>
I have heard so many Christians say, "I am believing God for (this)" and "I believed God for (that)." And I look at the results in their life, seeing no evidence of their faith. You can usually tell by a person's confession what they truly believe because out of their heart their mouth will speak (Matthew 12:34). I have come to understand that these people "hoped" that God would answer them, but they weren't truly "believing."

As we said in the last chapter, faith is *confident expectation*. When you truly believe God's Word and *know* that what you believe will come to pass, that is faith. Faith is not believing God *can* do it, it is believing that God *will* do it...or better yet...that He *did* do it because His Word says so. Faith is not *hoping* everything will turn out for the best. Now, you cannot have faith without hope, for faith is the "substance of things hoped for" (Hebrews 11:1), but faith is much more than mere hope.

When my wife became pregnant with our second child, she was believing God for a supernatural childbirth. She wanted an all-natural, medicine-free delivery. She was also believing God for a 3-hour labor, and to labor during the day so that she would not lose a night's sleep (she had lost 2 nights with our first child). And on top of this, we decided to have the child at home. Our experience with the birth of our first child was less than spectacular, and we knew that our covenant granted us better rewards.

Louise immersed herself in the Word. She found Scriptures that spoke to the very situation she was facing and stood upon them firmly. She later told me that in the last few weeks of the pregnancy, she was so confident in what God was going to do in our pregnancy, it was like it had already happened. It was like she was just waiting for time to catch up with what she had already experienced! Friends, that is not hope! That is confidence! That is faith!

Faith Is Not Hypnosis
One day I was praying for someone, and I noticed that the whole time they were muttering over and over again (with their eyes closed), "I believe...I believe...I believe..." It seemed as though they were trying to hypnotize themselves into believing God's promise. When you truly understand and believe the promises that are spelled out in God's Word, you will not have to "trick" yourself into trusting and receiving from Him. You will not have to convince your mind. You will simply be "confidently expectant" in God, based on His Word.

Faith Is Not Wavering
Faith is based on God's Word. God's Word never wavers or changes. Therefore, our faith should never change other than to constantly be growing. I once knew someone who was "believing" God for their healing. Later, they were "believing" God for skilled surgeons. I am sorry to say this, but if they were truly *believing* for their healing, they would have been healed, because *true* faith works every time, and it always accomplishes what it sets out to accomplish. This person was in *hope*, not in faith.

A Year of Prosperity

Faith Is Not Having *Faith in Your Faith*

This goes back to the principle that faith is not hypnosis. In Mark 11:22, Jesus said, "Have faith in God." He never said, "Have faith in your faith." Faith is birthed out of an understanding of God's character, based on what His Word says. When we understand Who God is, and consequently, who we truly are in Christ, we will have faith in Him. And it is faith in Him—*not* faith in *our faith*—that produces results in our lives.

Faith Is Not Asking or Begging God To Do It

Faith is believing that God already did everything He needed to do. We do not need to ask God to heal us, for He already did 2000 years ago. All we need to do is freely receive what He already paid the price for. Jesus never *prayed* for someone to be healed. He commanded them to be healed. Then He gave us the same authority that He walked in and told us that we could do "greater works" than He did (John 14:12).

We need not ask or beg God to prosper us, for we already know that it is His Will to do so. We just need to believe and receive what He has already done on our behalf.

But I suppose that the most important thing to understand about what faith is not, is that faith is *not* ever going to fail to produce!

Chapter 49

The Covenant of Faith
Part 3: How Faith Works

> **Mark 11:22-24 (NIV)**
> *22 "Have faith in God," Jesus answered.*
> *23 "I tell you the truth, if anyone says to this mountain, 'Go, throw yourself into the sea,' and does not doubt in his heart but believes that what he says will happen, it will be done for him.*
> *24 Therefore I tell you, whatever you ask for in prayer, believe that you have received it, and it will be yours.*

One key to successfully put faith to work is to know that faith can not exist with doubt. You must believe what you say will happen. Some people think this is a difficult concept to grasp, but when you know and trust the promises that are in God's Word, doubt has a harder time creeping in.

Another key to understand is that our authority is in our mouth. In verse 23, Jesus said that we must "say" to the mountain...and that we must believe what we "say" will happen. As we have read previously, death and life are in our tongue.

Genesis 1 shows us that when God created man, he "breathed" into him the breath of life. Out of all of God's creations, man was the only being that received God's breath. Why is this significant? Because it takes breath to speak! God breathed His breath into man so that man could use the breath of God to speak with authority in the earth. We should

A Year of Prosperity

use this authority to speak blessing, provision, and whatever we need or want into our lives.

Mark 11:24 tells us that we receive when we pray...not when the prayer is answered, but when we pray. Then, after we have received, it will be ours. In other words, there is a period of time between the "Amen!" and the *answer.* The important thing to understand is that we receive it when we pray. The fact that we do not see it yet is immaterial, because faith is not based on what is seen. Faith is the evidence of things "not seen."

In chapter 41 of this book I recounted part of a true story about a man who went deep-sea fishing for Blue Marlin. But I did not share the key of how he achieved his success that day. This is a wonderful example of how to put faith to work:

This man and another Christian friend had chartered a fishing boat in Hawaii. They told the captain and his crew that they wanted to catch a Blue Marlin. The captain assured him that Blue Marlins were not anywhere close to that area during that time of year. Blue Marlins were supposed to be hundreds of miles away. But this did not discourage the man's faith.

After several hours of fishing, they had caught several fish but no Blue Marlins. The man's friend could see that he was starting to lose heart. So the friend said to him, "Hey buddy! According to Mark 11:24, when did you receive your Blue Marlin? When you prayed, or when it shows up?" He answered, "When I prayed." Within a minute or so, the man had a fish on the line. When they finally reeled it in, they discovered that it was a Blue Marlin! The captain and his crew were hysterical, jumping up and down, cheering and shouting! They were almost in disbelief that something so miraculous could happen.

Use your faith to receive whatever you are in need of according to God's Word. You will receive the same way this man did...when you pray, *not* when it shows up.

Chapter 50

The Covenant of Faith
Part 4: How Faith Is Built

> **Romans 10:17 (KJV)**
> *So then faith cometh by hearing, and hearing by the word of God.*

As I have said many times before in this book, faith ultimately comes from the Word. If you want to build your faith, you must stay in the Word of God. Just as my wife did during her pregnancy, we must immerse ourselves in God's Word. Knowing what His Word says will build our trust and faith in Him. Our understanding of His character as a provider and rewarder will grow. Consequently, so will our faith.

Whenever I pray for people, I try to make it a habit to ask them what Scripture they are standing on. This is a great way to specifically identify where their faith is located. If faith is built on God's Word, then a person who is truly in faith will have no trouble telling you what promise of the Word they are claiming.

A pastor friend of mine had a lady come to him for prayer during a church service. She had been a chain smoker for about fifty years, and she had lung cancer. The doctors had tracked a growth in her lungs for over 18 months. They were going to operate on her in the next few weeks. The pastor asked her what Word she was standing on. She did not have an answer.

A Year of Prosperity

Rather than praying for her, he sent her home with some literature on healing Scriptures. He told her to read the literature and study the Scriptures so that her faith would be built. How many times do we say useless prayers with no faith behind them? This pastor did not want to pray for this woman because he knew she was not yet ready to receive. This is very significant that he refused to pray for her because the woman was the pastor's aunt!

Two weeks later, she returned to the church. She had studied the Word and was now ready to receive her healing. The church prayed for her and her cancer was totally healed. She went to the doctor that week, and they were astonished to find that the cancer they had been tracking for 18 months was totally gone!

This woman had thought that the pastor's faith would heal her. But the pastor knew that Jesus said that "our" faith will make us whole—not someone else's faith.

You should also know that one promise in God's Word is enough to stand on. You don't have to have the whole Bible memorized in order to have faith. When my wife was pregnant, she stood on four Scriptures. Those verses were enough to carry her through a supernatural childbirth. And I must say that her labor and delivery was one of the most anointed and miraculous things I have ever experienced.

Louise's faith regarding pregnancy and childbirth was based on four promises in Scripture. I will list them here along with notes that she wrote to herself to encourage her faith (in parentheses):

- Galatians 3:13 – Christ has redeemed us from the curse of the law. (I have the right to give birth with ease, quickly, and pain-free.)
- Exodus 1:19 – the Hebrew women are not as the Egyptian women; for they are lively, and are delivered before the

A Year of Prosperity

midwives come unto them. (I deliver as the Hebrew women, quickly, and with strength.)

- Ephesians 3:20 – Now unto him that is able to do exceeding abundantly above all that we ask or think, according to the power that works in us. (The Lord is continually exceeding my expectations, so I receive that, during my delivery and recovery, the Lord will go above and beyond all that I have spoken and prayed.)
- Psalm 127:3 – the fruit of the womb is His reward (I will bless the Lord as I give birth.)

The principles of faith work for whatever you need. For us, we applied them during Louise's pregnancy. She specifically believed God for a 3-hour labor (3 hours from transition to birth). She also specifically believed God for a labor that would not rob her of a night's sleep. In other words, she did not want to labor through the night, but rather during the day.

She claimed all of this and spoke it into existence with the authority she has as a believer. She went into labor on a Sunday morning. I went to church and led worship, then I came home immediately after worship. After church, several ladies from the church came over to pray with us as Louise labored. We played games, went for walks, ate and laughed. At 9:30 p.m., Louise went into transition (the intense part of labor). By 12:25 a.m., she was ready to push. She pushed twice, and Caleb was born!

Louise got her 3-hour labor, and did not lose a night's sleep. She did not need medication, nor did she need stitches. She stood on the Word of God, she knew what her promises were, and her faith produced the results she sought.

Faith is like a muscle. It must be exercised in order to strengthen. A wise man once said, "Don't try to believe God for a wedding cake, until you have first believed him for a donut." Building your faith is a process. The reason faith-building is a process is because we are so trained in this society to trust in what we can see. But faith is trusting in

A Year of Prosperity

what you cannot see. Faith is trusting in an unseen God for unseen promises. Faith has eyes, but unlike our natural eyes, faith's eyes see the unseen.

Faith is based on truth, not on fact. The *fact* may be that your checkbook is "in the red," but the *truth* is that God will supply all your needs according to His riches in glory by Christ Jesus (Philippians 4:19). The *fact* may be that your body is showing symptoms of sickness, malady, or disease, but the *truth* is that by His stripes you were healed (1 Peter 2:24). Fact is based on the seen, but truth is based on the Word. And faith is based on truth.

Chapter 51

The Covenant of Faith
Part 5: Faith and Works

> **James 2:14-18 (NKJV)**
> *[14] What does it profit, my brethren, if someone says he has faith but does not have works? Can faith save him?*
> *[15] If a brother or sister is naked and destitute of daily food,*
> *[16] and one of you says to them, "Depart in peace, be warmed and filled," but you do not give them the things which are needed for the body, what does it profit?*
> *[17] Thus also faith by itself, if it does not have works, is dead.*
> *[18] But someone will say, "You have faith, and I have works." Show me your faith without your works, and I will show you my faith by my works.*

A few years ago, a worship leader friend of mine named Gary got kidney disease in one of his kidneys. The kidney was shutting down. He was put on dialysis 3 to 4 days a week, along with about twenty-five prescription medications. His diet was extremely limited, and his weekly routine greatly inhibited his career as a restaurant owner. His health problems also affected his ability to lead worship on Sunday mornings. His doctor put him on a donor list, but the likelihood of finding a donor before the kidney completely shut down was not very promising.

One day he got fed up. He told his wife, "Either God's Word is true or it's not. Either God is my healer or He's not. Either

A Year of Prosperity

this whole thing called Christianity is true and good, or we are all wasting our time." He marched upstairs into his bathroom, grabbed all of his medications, and threw them in the trash.

He called his doctor and told him what he had done. He then explained that he was not coming in for dialysis anymore. The doctor said, "Gary, you will be dead in 2 weeks." Gary said, "No, I won't; my God is my healer." Within 2-3 days, Gary was totally fine. He could eat whatever he wanted, and his life was back to normal.

Gary's "works" that identified his faith was the act of throwing his medications in the trash. My wife's "works" that accompanied her faith was her option to stay home and have a baby in a peaceful home environment rather than a hospital. I do not know what works you may need to do to activate your faith, but true faith is not intimidated to act.

Gary's faith was ready to throw all of his medications away, but some people are not there yet in their faith walk. You will have to determine where your faith is in order to determine what works will need to be applied. As quoted before, don't believe God for a wedding cake until you have believed him for a donut.

I have another friend in ministry who wants to stop taking several of her medications. I first asked her what Scripture she was standing on. She could not tell me. Therefore, I knew she was not at a place in her faith where she could discontinue her medications—"cold turkey." I told her to get in the Word and find some Scriptures that apply to her situation then gradually stop taking the medications. She needed to *exercise* her faith and build that *muscle* a bit before she tried *lifting anything heavy*.

Know that your faith is null and void without works to activate it, for faith without works is dead. Whatever you need to accompany your faith is between you and God. Pray and

A Year of Prosperity

trust God to show you how to activate your faith with your works.

Chapter 52

We Will Always Depend On God

There is so much to be said about Biblical prosperity. I feel that this book has just scratched the surface on the matter, but I want to leave you with just one more thought about God's design for your finances.

There are those who want God to prosper them in order to take away the pressure of life. And it stands to reason that with plenty of finances, pressures would be relieved. As we stated, money answers all things (Ecclesiastes 10:19). But we also need to acknowledge that with more money comes more responsibility. To whom much is given, much is required (Luke 12:48).

Some people want God to prosper them to the point that they will not have to use their faith anymore. But as the Bible says in several passages, "The just shall live by faith." We will always need to exercise our faith. And as we do so, our faith as well as our relationship with God will grow.

We will always depend on God. God will never prosper us to the point that we will no longer have to rely on Him. He will never bring us to a place that will drive us farther from Him. That would be detrimental to us, therefore detrimental to the Kingdom.

This is why it has been stated many times in this book that prosperity comes from seeking God, not from seeking money. If we seek His Kingdom first, all of the things we need in life will be added to us. We cannot serve God and

A Year of Prosperity

serve money (Matthew 6:24). But in serving God, we will not need to serve money because God will prosper us.

In your quest for Biblical prosperity, remember to always keep your priorities straight. Money is wonderful and answers all things, but nothing is worth more than your relationship with God. Nothing is worth sacrificing your marriage, your relationship with your family or your kids. Nothing is worth giving up your joy, your peace or your sanity.

So trust God to meet every one of your needs—whether they be spiritual, physical, emotional, mental, relational, or financial. You have a covenant with God...a covenant of provision for everything you need in life, a covenant of goodness and one that grants us victory in every area of our life. All we have to do is receive it by faith.

This never-ending dependence is His design—by His Sovereign Authority and Will. All we have to lead us in life is God's Spirit and His Word. And how sweet it is to go on living with the revelation that His Spirit and His Word are <u>much</u>, <u>much more</u> than we will ever need!

God's best for your success!

Prosperity Scriptures

The following are Scriptures for you to study to help build and strengthen your faith. All Scripture references that were used in this book are listed here. The list is in book order from Genesis to Revelation. There are many other Scriptures regarding finances in the Bible, but only the ones used in this book are listed here. Study them often.

Old Testament
- **Genesis**
  1:11-12 | 3:16-19 | 13:5-9 | 14:20 | Chapters 29-31
- **Exodus**
  1:19 | Chap. 4 | Chap. 16
- **Deuteronomy**
  15:6 | 23:19, 20 | 28:2-8 | 28:9-14
- **2 Samuel** – Chapter 6
- **1 Kings** – Chapter 17
- **1 Chronicles** – Chapter 17
- **2 Chronicles** – 20:15
- **Psalms**
  8:2 | 22:3 | Chap. 23 | 33:12 | 37:4 | 103:2, 5 | 112:5 | 127:3
  133:3
- **Proverbs**
  4:6 | 4:23 | 6:2 | 10:22 | 13:22 | 14:20 | 18:21, 22 | 22:7 | 23:7
  Chapter 31
- **Ecclesiastes** – 10:19
- **Isaiah** – Chapter 61
- **Daniel** – Chapter 6
- **Amos** – 3:3
- **Malachi**
  2:13-16 | 3:8-12

New Testament
- **Matthew**

A Year of Prosperity

5:28 | Chapter 6 | 7:11 | 10:41 | 12:34 | Chapter 14 | 17:24-27 | 19:4-6 | 19:23, 24 & 26 | Chapter 22

- <u>Mark</u>
  6:41-43 | 8:7, 8 | 8:19-21 | 10:29, 30 | 11:22-24 | Chapter 12
- <u>Luke</u>
  4:18 | Chapter 5 | 6:27-35 | 6:38 | 7:23 | 12:48 | Chapter 20
- <u>John</u>
  3:16 | 8:32 | 14:12 | 16:23b & 24 | Chapter 21
- <u>Acts</u>
  13:22 | Chapter 16
- <u>Romans</u>
  8:16 | 10:17
- <u>1 Corinthians</u> – 1:27
- <u>2 Corinthians</u>
  1:20 | Chapter 6 | Chapter 9
- <u>Galatians</u>
  Chapter 3 | 5:22 & 23 | 6:9
- <u>Ephesians</u>
  2:8,9 | 3:20 | 5:8
- <u>Philippians</u> – 4:19
- <u>1 Timothy</u>
  6:9,10 | 6:17, 18
- <u>Hebrews</u>
  11:1, 6
- <u>James</u>
  1:7, 8 | 1:17 | 2:14-18 | 4:3
- <u>1 Peter</u>
  2:24 | 5:7, 8
- <u>1 John</u> – 3:1,2